P9-EDF-172

ALSO BY MARILYN FRENCH

My Summer with George

Our Father

The War Against Women

Her Mother's Daughter

Beyond Power

Shakespeare's Division of Experience

The Bleeding Heart

The Women's Room

The Book as World: James Joyce's "Ulysses"

A SEASON IN HELL

A SEASON

IN

HELL

A MEMOIR

MARILYN FRENCH

ALFRED A. KNOPF · NEW YORK · 1998

THIS IS A BORZOI BOOK
PUBLISHED BY ALFRED A. KNOPF, INC.

Copyright © 1998 by Belles Lettres, Inc.

www.randomhouse.com

Library of Congress Cataloging-in-Publication Data

French, Marilyn.
A season in hell : a memoir / by Marilyn French. — 1st ed.
p.   cm.
ISBN 0-679-45509-4
1. French, Marilyn —Biography.
2. Women novelists, American—20th century—Biography.
3. Esophagus—Cancer—Patients—United States—Biography.
4. Near-death experiences—United States. I. Title.
PS3556.R42Z467   1998
813'.54—dc21   98-14575   CIP   [B]

Manufactured in the United States of America

First Edition

To Jamie French,
Rob French,
and Barbara McKechnie,
who went through it
with me

Love seeketh not itself to please,
Nor for itself hath any care,
But for another gives its ease,
And builds a Heaven in Hell's despair.
                              —William Blake

CONTENTS

A SEASON IN HELL

1992

MARCH—JUNE

Saturday morning, March 7, 1992, was bright and
sunny on the east coast of Florida. It would be hot,
I thought, but I dressed formally in a pantsuit and
heels, because I was scheduled to address a local chapter of NOW that day. I live alone, so did not talk to
anyone until I reached the restaurant where I was to
speak and was greeted by the NOW people. Then I
was startled to hear a thin, reedy sound emerge from
my throat. It was not my voice at all. I was puzzled; my
daughter, Jamie, had returned to New York the day
before, after a week's visit. Although I had had what I
thought was laryngitis while she was with me, my voice
had been normal. Now it was not.

Mike Edmondson, a friend, came up to greet me. I
was surprised to see him—few men attend NOW
events. But Mike is political and a feminist. I recalled

that we had been supposed to see a movie together some weeks earlier but somehow had not done so.

"Wonderful to see you, Mike! How have you been?"

"Not too good, Marilyn. That's why I never called. The Monday after you came for dinner, I was diagnosed with cancer."

I felt myself pale.

"Testicular cancer. They operated. It's gone. I'm fine."

It was almost inconceivable that he could be diagnosed and cured within so brief a time. "It seems miraculous," I said.

"That's how they treat it now." He smiled. Mike is a good-looking man in his thirties, and he shone with health. It was equally shocking that he should develop cancer and that he had been cured of it in the few weeks since I'd seen him.

As we discussed his treatment, I thought about my friend Sibyl Claiborne. I had flown up to New York in February to appear on a PEN panel on Taboos in Literature, which she chaired. Sibyl had seen her oncologist that same day and, in quiet distress, told me she had been diagnosed with cancer of the lung. The doctors at NYU Hospital told her it was tiny, smaller than a quarter, and that she had a good prognosis. As she recounted this, a pang of dread struck me, hard, like a gong in my chest. I began to say that I, too, had cancer, but I stopped myself in time. I didn't have cancer. Why did I feel that I did? Since the fall of 1991, I had had an intermittent consciousness of—or had been inventing—a deep-seated malaise in my body. In November I had had a flu that hung on for months, then turned into a cold, which as late as March had not yet gone away. I told myself my dread at hearing Sibyl's news was just empathy. Maybe I wanted to share her grief, since I was so fond of her and regretted the sorrow she bore—her husband had died a couple of years earlier and her only child, a son, had died of AIDS the year before. She had no family left; she had only her close friend Grace Paley.

Maybe what was driving me was guilt at the fact that I was still smoking. I had been smoking since I was fifteen, since the night of the junior prom in the Café Rouge of the old Hotel Pennsylvania. I was an instant addict, moving swiftly up to a pack a day forty-six years ago. For years, doctors and friends urged me to quit, but I rationalized. There was no cancer on either side of my family, and beyond that, I couldn't believe that an activity I enjoyed so much could harm me. My brilliant uncle Henry (who also smoked and drank) regularly told me stories of relatives of his (always men) who had smoked two packs of cigarettes and drunk a fifth of bourbon every day until they died at ninety-four. I counted on being like them.

But today, listening to Mike, although he was recovered and out of danger, I felt the dread again. And now I had a symptom. Dread became constant, like the sound of a drone, a repetitive, dull bass instrument used in medieval music. Sometimes its voice seems to vanish, overpowered by the other instruments, but it is continually present in the background, a grinding presence, grindingly the same.

I gave my speech with my half-voice, which didn't clear that day or the next. After ten days I called my New York internist, Edith Langner, the doctor I trusted

more than any other, and told her this symptom had
followed a lingering cold. She prescribed an antibiotic
and told me to call her the following week. The next
week, the voice remained the same. I had no other
symptoms. Hypothesizing that it was an allergy, she
recommended a nasal spray. But I was convinced I had
throat cancer.

A busy and exciting year lay ahead. For the past seven
years, seven days a week, nine to ten hours a day, I had
been researching and writing a history of women. It
had become a huge project, edging out all others. I had
not published a new book since 1986, had not earned
an advance since 1985, and the history was still unfinished. But I was near the end. After hundreds of pages
describing the constrictions placed on women in past
ages, I had written a segment on how law and custom
treat women in the present, the twentieth century. Once
I compiled it, I found this segment so shocking that I
felt it should be published separately right away. I took
the title of the segment, *The War Against Women,* for the
book, which my usual publishers at home and abroad
were eager to publish. It would be issued in several
countries in March and April 1992, and I had promised
to promote it in England, Ireland, Germany, Holland,
and the United States. I looked forward to traveling
abroad, seeing old friends and familiar places, and to
being on the move again after so many sedentary years.
I would travel, speak in bookstores, meet new people—
things I enjoyed but hadn't done in a long time.

On March 19, I flew to New York and, at Dr.
Langner's direction, went for a chest X ray. She had

nagged me about smoking ever since I first consulted her, and clearly she was worried about lung cancer now. But the X ray showed my lungs were clear.

The night before I left on my tour, my coven celebrated the spring equinox. The coven was born when Gloria Steinem invited E. M. (Esther) Broner, Carol Jenkins, and me for dinner one night in 1988. *Ms.* having been (temporarily) sold to two Australian feminists, Gloria had fewer responsibilities than usual; for the first time in many years, she had some leisure time and decided to use it to do things she wanted to do instead of things she had to do. This included seeing women she wished to know better. She also wanted to form a group to celebrate, not traditional holidays, but their ancient equivalents, the solstices and equinoxes. We decided to call ourselves a coven, modeling ourselves on ancient cells of witches, wise women with healing powers in medieval Europe. Over the years, we became intimate friends—not in the sense that we spoke every day and knew every detail of the others' lives, but as friends who knew each other's qualities and had a sense of each other's fears and longings, the grooves and velvet folds we were trapped in, our efforts to pull ourselves free; and we were ardent about one another's well-being. These women were (and are) among my most important friends. The first meeting was held at Gloria's house. I don't recall our discussion that first night; we sat down to dinner at eight and rose at three in the morning. We all felt that this was something that should continue and, in future meetings, used the same satisfying form we had arrived at the first time.

The day after the March 1992 coven meeting, I boarded a plane for London.

My trip was deeply satisfying. Throughout Britain and Germany, I spoke in bookstores thronged with people (mostly women) who were as shocked and appalled as I by the condition of women in general and who kept asking me and each other what they could do to make a difference. In Dublin, my friend the writer Lois Gould came in from County Mayo to have dinner with me—Dublin has lots of fine restaurants nowadays—and we had great fun together, as we always do. I spoke at University College and went with some lively Irish feminists to have tea with Mary Robinson, then the President of Ireland, in her mansion on Howth Hill. She had asked to meet me (we had encountered each other at a party in County Mayo the year she campaigned for office, but she had not recognized my name at the time). I admire Ms. Robinson greatly: she devised ways to use a powerless and limited office to articulate a strong and positive moral position. Her meeting with me caused the conservative newspapers, which had taken horrified note of my visit to Ireland, to bray in outrage on the front page.

After more promotion in England, I flew to Germany, where I was scheduled to give a speech every night and several interviews a day for a week. The reward for this terrible grind was that my publishers put me up at some of the most exquisite hotels I have ever seen (especially in Cologne, where the French doors of my antique-filled suite faced the cathedral across the street). I moved from Bonn to Frankfurt,

Düsseldorf, and Cologne, then flew to Munich, a new city to me. From there I was going to Berlin and then home. My German publisher, Claudia Vidoni, accompanied me on this tour and, on my one free afternoon, took me for a walk through Munich.

Knowing its history, I was stiff viewing the quaintest of the German cities I had visited (I'd been *through* but not *in* the east, except for Berlin). I asked to see the square where Hitler held his first rallies. Its entrance was marked by an old monument, which Hitler converted to a Nazi shrine. People passing it were required to give the Nazi salute on pain of death, Claudia said. The monument still stands, rededicated to new ideals. I stood there for a long time, overcome. My throat was thick; I could not speak; I felt a little dizzy. What filled my brain was an overwhelming sense of a complex idea that came all at once, like a huge map the eye apprehends in one moment: the thought of the agony that began here, in this charming, quaint old town, and moved to Berlin, where I would fly tomorrow morning. It was a short flight; it took Hitler far longer to progress from Munich to Berlin, but that was where he, too, moved. And Stalin, too, moved toward Berlin; that was where they met, the monstrous machine set in motion by Hitler and the monstrous machine set in motion by Stalin. Two men, two mere mortals: the fruit of their lives intertwined in Berlin. I had not been there since the wall fell, but I had once walked along the ugly thing, staring into the rubble of East Berlin that lined it.

It was just a line on a map, almost a straight line, north-northeast, the direction I would take tomorrow. I saw Hitler massing support in Munich, entering Berlin and taking over that grand imperial city with its palaces and parks, its linden trees and beautiful allées and magnificent apartments, its magisterial architecture and down-and-dirty cabarets. Stalin rose in Russia over the slaughter of the civil war, millions of bleeding bodies dying in the snow, then killed millions more on his own. They made a pact my uncle Henry claimed would be invincible: Germany had industry, Russia was rich in raw materials; together they were unbeatable, he insisted. But they blew it. Two men, two opposing philosophies, but identical twins in despotism and terror. Both anti-Semitic, if truth be told. Between them, how many humans did they destroy? Jews across Europe traveling in sealed boxcars to unspeakable camps that no one can be said to have survived (for those who outlived them were tragically damaged and passed their grief on to another generation). And Stalin's paranoiac campaigns. And the war itself. How many millions of humans does that make?

I saw this simple line, Munich to Berlin, like a deep gash in the body of the continent, and blood spreading out from it in all directions, covering the continent and beyond, moving like a tidal wave across the world, leaving no one untouched by grief and injury.

Now the wall was down, the camps were memorials, it was all over (except that Nazism was rising again, right here in the city where it began). The destruction of the wall was an event they could hold ceremonies about, like the Pope and the Archbishop of Canterbury having tea (as they did some years ago), their churches' slaughters and burnings and drawings-and-quarterings and excommunications and inquisitions and witch hunts and anathemas and tirades, which swept Europe for two centuries, over in the late twentieth century. Hey, let's do tea.

I could not speak. I could barely walk back to my hotel. I was overwhelmed by a sense of futility and weariness at the murderousness of my race. I felt I was dying, and wanted to die.

At the same time, I was amazed at myself. This was, after all, hardly the first time I had thought about these two men, or the history in which they were embedded. Nor was I in the habit of feeling overwhelmed and maudlin about historical events long past. I wondered what I was doing, why I was letting myself down this way into a well of despair—why I was so emotional.

I flew to Berlin next day for a full schedule of events. The following day, I was to leave Germany. I had a 7:00 a.m. TV appearance, inadvertently causing a hysterical brouhaha because I had worn a royal-blue dress and they had a royal-blue cloth backing on the set. The director insisted that a different curtain be found, refused to start filming until it was. I was growing nervous—I had to pick up my luggage at the hotel before catching my plane. In the end, I had two hours to spare before my noon flight. I had my driver take me past what had been Checkpoint Charlie into East Berlin. Entering East Berlin had always been an ordeal, whether one went by car, bus, train, or subway. Now we simply drove through the gate.

Although much of socialist East Berlin had been left to rot, especially around the wall, there was, farther in, a charm and peacefulness the West lacked. The West was a gigantic ad for stuff, a clamoring competition in neon stretching its neck as high as possible so as to be seen in the East, selling the virtues of cameras and cars, television sets and radios. East Berlin was in many ways a quiet little town. Blocks of apartments were lined with trees; there were few cars, few shops (and no neon signs), and few people. It was quiet, unmanicured. Now that the wall was down, there was construction everywhere—huge cranes, rutted streets, rot revealed. The work might lead to a richer future, but the place was raw at the moment.

When I boarded the plane for my trip home, I thought I had never before in my life been so tired. My fatigue felt serious, like the fatigue of illness. I told the cabin assistants not to wake me for dinner, and slept all the way back.

I had no time to recover, however. As soon as I landed, I was launched into promotion in New York, speaking at *Newsday*'s Book and Author Luncheon in the Brooklyn Botanic Garden and giving print and TV interviews. Dr. Langner examined me and found nothing wrong, but she recommended an ear, nose, and throat specialist. I made an appointment with him for May 4, two weeks off, then continued to do promotion. I spoke at Sarah Lawrence College, did a host of radio and TV interviews. On Shakespeare's birthday, April 23, I flew to Terre Haute to speak on *Measure for Measure* at Indiana State University. The following week, I had interviews in Washington, D.C., and spoke at the Smithsonian. Next I flew to Boston, and late Friday I returned to New York.

On Monday, May 4, I saw the ENT specialist. Like

Edie, he diagnosed an allergy, and prescribed the same nasal spray. I told him it had not helped. He said I wasn't using it properly and gave me new instructions. I happily accepted this correction, even though my drone was sawing through everything he said. The week after, I flew to Philadelphia, then Toronto, where I addressed a large crowd at the university. I was introduced by Michele Landsberg, the brilliant columnist for the *Toronto Star*. Michele, a friend of Esther Broner's, has become a friend of mine as well; she joined me for dinner, bringing a group of lively, warm people. Dinners like this, with intelligent, engaging conversation, were major joys in my life. I briefly forgot my dread.

On Mother's Day, my kids took me for brunch in SoHo, but the dread was back. I knew I was not well. The sense that I had cancer hung upon me like an invisible black veil that only I was aware of, even though it occasionally occurred to me that I was inventing it. I said nothing; I was just silently terrified, unable to explain the malaise that permeated my being. Since I did not feel legitimate in speaking about it, I hardly spoke at all. Like a lover obsessed with someone married or otherwise unsuitable, I could not talk about what occupied me, but could think of nothing else. I walked through interviews and speeches like a zombie. I gave a talk at the YWCA in New York, did some interviews, and then flew to Chicago for more readings and interviews. At the end of the week I received an honorary degree from Hofstra, my undergraduate alma mater, and gave a speech; even there, I felt isolated with my terrible secret, enervated. The next week, there were more interviews, and a book party at the lovely town house of my agent, Charlotte Sheedy. A week later, I flew out to the West Coast for more promotion.

Early in June, I went to Boston for the semiannual meeting of the Harvard Graduate Society Council, an informal body intended mainly to keep graduate alumni involved with the university. As I was dressing for dinner at my Cambridge hotel, for some reason I placed my fingertips on the soft tissue just above the clavicle on the left side of my chest. I felt two small, hard lumps. The dread leaped up, then fell still. What had been only a feeling was now fact.

This trip being at my own expense, I could take some time for personal pursuits. I wanted to see Barbara Greenberg, a close friend for almost thirty years. Barbara, a poet who lives in Boston, offered to drive me around Lincoln, where I had set *Our Father,* the novel I was writing. I had often visited that beautiful town during my years at Harvard, but I needed more detailed background for the novel. Barbara and I spent a grand day visiting churches and gazing at mansions.

Barbara's husband, Harold, is a surgeon, and over the decades of her marriage she has picked up considerable medical knowledge. So as we relaxed over drinks at her house, I asked her to feel the lumps and tell me what she thought. She did; she frowned and said, "Show them to Harold tonight." Harold came in as we were about to go out to dinner, and I repeated my request. He felt them, frowned, also said, "Show them to your doctor." The concern and dismay they tried to hide reinforced my sense that the lumps were cancer.

As soon as I returned to New York, I made an appointment with the ENT physician I had seen before.

He ordered a CT scan. As I was leaving his office, he said, "I am very sorry for you, Ms. French." I deduced he didn't need a CT scan to know cancer when he felt it. The scan, taken on Thursday, June 11, showed a growth on my esophagus. I was given the results on Friday.

Sick at heart, I flew to Dublin on Sunday, to give the keynote address at the Joyce Symposium. I love Ireland, and I've walked through Dublin often, on Bloomsdays and other visits; and this was to be a special visit—President Mary Robinson was to introduce me. But after giving my speech and attending the Bloomsday Banquet (at Trinity this year, rather than Dublin Castle), I left. I did not stay to enjoy the city or the rest of the symposium, as I usually do. I was too anxious and frightened, and I needed to make plans for treatment.

The day after I returned, I went to St. Luke's–Roosevelt for a biopsy conducted by the ENT specialist. He called even before the sample had been biopsied. There was no question in his mind: the mass in my esophagus was malignant. He wanted to operate, to get rid of it as soon as possible; how about Monday? The idea that he could rid me of this cancer that easily and quickly very much appealed to me, and I agreed. But I also called Edie Langner, who said that was rushing things. Wait, she advised. Consult other doctors. I'll get some names for you.

On Friday, the next day, I was supposed to fly to Stratford, Ontario, to give a talk at the Shakespeare Theatre Festival, but the biopsy had left my throat too sore for speech. I realized this on Thursday afternoon, a little late to find a replacement. I felt terrible at letting the Stratford people down, especially at the last minute, and searched my mind. Then it came to me: Gloria! It didn't matter that she wasn't a Shakespeare scholar; everyone would love meeting the most famous feminist in the world, who is also a graceful, intelligent speaker and a lovely person. If she was free, if she was willing, she could give the speech I'd written—if she wanted to use it. She might even enjoy it: I had analyzed *Measure for Measure* with special attention to its several endings, in which two wronged women clamor for justice. Both have been harmed by Antonio, the surrogate for the true ruler, the Duke, who has been away. The women charge Antonio with what we would call sexual harassment and rape. But what is astonishing is that the arguments Antonio and the Duke (acting as male authority) use to silence and dismiss the women are exactly the same as those used by the men of the Senate committee against Anita Hill during the Clarence Thomas hearings.

I called Gloria, who said she was pleased to do this, especially since I had never before asked her for anything. Not a word about her rare free weekend sacrificed, or the fact that she would have to leave for Canada the very next day. She went and was, of course, a sensation; the Stratford audience and officials were delighted. On top of that, she donated the entire honorarium to a cause she supports. This is one example of why so many people consider her a saint.

The biopsy showed I had squamous cell cancer, a slow-growing type that grows in organ linings. I later discovered that the mass the ENT man found was not the primary cancer but a *metastasis*. Edie had saved me from a terrible error. If the ENT specialist had operated on the tumor he found, he would not have removed the entire cancer and might have damaged my voice box, since the cancer was touching the nerve leading to the vocal cord. I never returned to that doctor.

The soreness in my throat faded in two days, and on Monday I went ahead with my plans to fly to Amsterdam for the 1992 Feminist Book Fair, where I was to speak. I enjoyed the week at the fair as much as I could enjoy anything in that time. I met Marleen Gorris (who in 1996 would win an Academy Award for *Antonia's Line* but who had already made the deeply impressive *A Question of Silence,* which many people believe to be the greatest feminist film ever made). I went through the motions of debating Fay Weldon (a dear woman with whom I have no significant differences). With my friends Annaville Petterson and Nettie Blanken, I walked out to Marken lighthouse, a beautiful spot on Lake Ysselmeer, the former Zuyder Zee. It was too long a walk for me, and I was grateful when we stopped for beer and sandwiches on the way back.

I was moving about in a kind of stupor, wondering if this was the last time I would see this friend or that, the last time I would visit this lovely city, the last time I would be an apparently healthy person in public. And indeed, that was the case.

1992

JULY

The day after my return from Amsterdam, I had another CT scan and began visiting oncologists. Edie recommended a lung specialist at Sloan-Kettering, an oncologist at Columbia Presbyterian, and a female oncologist in private practice. My children accompanied me, to help me decide among them. The Sloan-Kettering doctor told me the mass that had been detected was not the primary cancer and that it was necessary to discover the primary site before treatment could proceed. He suspected it was in the lung, but he could not find it on my chest X rays or CT scan.

All of these doctors treated me like a responsible, intelligent person. None of them was able to spot the primary site of the cancer on my X rays, which I now carried with me (Sloan-Kettering had lost my first set). Still, they made very different impressions on me. The

Columbia oncologist, an extremely likable man, seemed so eager to make me better that he felt sure he could do so rather easily. He shrugged off the problem of the primary site too cheerfully to arouse my confidence. The oncologist in private practice could not get past her annoyance at our lateness (Jamie and I had been stuck in traffic for half an hour). She showed no interest in my case, or in how to find the primary site, and was completely pessimistic about my chances of survival. The S-K lung specialist, Elliot Strong, was kind and met my eyes when either of us spoke. Beyond that, he would do something that made me trust and respect him deeply.

During the weeks when I visited doctors, I was rarely alone. Someone or several people—one or more of my children, Charlotte Sheedy, Esther Broner, Gloria Steinem, LeAnne Schreiber, Barbara Greenberg—went with me to all my doctors' appointments, CT scans, the biopsy; one or two came to have dinner with me every night. On July 2, the coven held a meeting, our usual solstice meeting, delayed because of my trip to Holland. It felt, however, like an emergency meeting dedicated to me.

At coven meetings we gather gradually, chat over drinks, then have a formal dinner. Candles are spread around the meeting place; the lights are low. After dinner we move to soft chairs, and then someone begins. She will describe a problem with which she needs help—finding direction toward some goal, or a personal transformation she wishes for but is not achieving. We listen intently; we try to rephrase what is said, to be sure we understand what is wanted, needed. Then we discuss the qualities necessary to reach the desired end. After that comes the magical part of the evening, as we surround the seeker and call down upon her head whatever she needs of spirit, courage, and clarity to accomplish her desire. I say this is magical because it feels enchanted: the wisher feels enveloped by goodwill and love; the givers feel empowered by a wave of largesse and love. And in truth, we have had some success in helping each other to fulfill desires and overcome difficulties.

This evening, my friends surrounded me with their bodies and spirits as if they were electrically charged. They changed the very air, calling on all benevolent energies and spirits to surround me, heal me.

The next day, my son, Rob, drove me to my country house. My head was not functioning properly; I felt so dazed that I feared I would have an accident if I tried to drive. The children—Jamie, Rob, and Barbara—had planned a large party that weekend. They called it a going-to-the-hospital Fourth of July party; I called it a farewell party. A host of my friends and my children's friends attended; the kids did the planning, shopping, cooking, and cleaning up. Many people stayed overnight, and at its end I felt surrounded by love and good wishes, deeply cared about, unusual for me.

Another week went by, and nothing happened. Edie calmly insisted that no one knew anything definite about cancer and no one could predict my future. She refused to assume either that I was doomed or that I would recover. But I was anxious: time was passing,

the cancer was growing, and no one was doing anything. I believed that no one would act unless I did
(shades of my childhood sense of total responsibility
for our family!), that the doctors were unsure and
therefore paralyzed. So I telephoned Dr. Strong, who
had most impressed me medically and humanly, saying
I was concerned about the delay and wanted some
action on my case. He told me to come in and see him.
Charlotte went with me.

What makes a doctor wonderful, beyond medical
competence, is one simple characteristic: understanding
of suffering, personal comprehension of pain. One
would think that anyone over thirty must know pain,
but in fact, men in our society are encouraged to
deny pain and suffering, and medical schools tend
to encourage such denial. As a result, many doctors,
women as well as men, become brittle and closed off.
Of course, they suffer—that is inevitable—but they
don't let themselves feel their suffering, so derive no
knowledge from it and cannot use it. And what we
deny ourselves, we deny others.

There are no special phrases or gestures needed to
communicate an understanding of pain (notwithstand-
ing our President's familiar "I feel your pain"). Those
who have it convey an implicit largeness of spirit and a
depth of feeling in utterance and gesture. For example,
a Mount Sinai nephrologist who attended me in 1995–96
would visit my hospital bed early in the morning—as
most doctors do. I do not rise early and was always
asleep when he arrived, around 8:00 a.m. But instead of
calling out sharply, "Ms. French!" and startling me
awake, as most doctors did, he would stand silently by

the side of the bed and lay his hand gently on my forehead. This would always wake me in the sweetest possible mood (a miraculous thing to induce in me in the morning!). I loved him for this gesture.

Dr. Strong was a man who understood pain. He reexamined the CT scan and shook his head again. He repeated that no one had been able to spot it, even using a magnifying glass. Then he said, "Ms. French, *you* know where the primary site is. You do. Think about it, and call me."

I did think about it, and after a time, I recalled sitting on my porch in the Berkshires the summer before, eating a sandwich made of a good Jewish rye bread with a crisp crust, and as I swallowed, the bread suddenly stuck in my throat. It felt as if it was passing over a swelling. At the time, my heart stopped and I thought: Oh, God! What is that? But I pushed the question away. It was nothing. If it was anything, it would make itself known in time, I told myself.

Now it had.

I called Dr. Strong and told him that the primary site was about two inches below my clavicle. He said he would pore over the X rays millimeter by millimeter with a magnifying glass. A few days later, he called, saying he had found a slight thickening exactly where I had said it would be.

Rob and my old Harvard friend LeAnne Schreiber went with me the next time. We had to wait four hours. Dr. Strong said he needed to perform a laryngoscopy and an endoscopic ultrasound to verify the location. I must have been distressed and shown it, because he insisted I wait and see Dr. McCormack, who would perform the endoscopy. Perhaps he thought seeing a woman would reassure me. (As I recall, I was upset mainly at being made to wait a total of seven hours that day.) A thoracic surgeon famed at S-K (and perhaps beyond), a former nun, the only female attending I ever met at S-K, Dr. Patricia McCormack was warm, direct, and nonofficious. She gave me the first (and only) words of hope I was to hear. Whatever kind of cancer I had, she said, it had been found early, was small and contained in a single area, and would be easily amenable to treatment *if* my body responded to chemotherapy.

Two days later, at some ghastly hour of the morning, Charlotte and I went to S-K for the procedure, performed under anesthesia. They found the primary tumor in the lining of the esophagus.

The prolonged search for the primary site of my cancer was the first in a series of events that cast me as an actor in my disease. Many patients receive a diagnosis as a prisoner receives a sentence: How many years? Death? The verdict / diagnosis feels like a judgment imposed by an indifferent authority. Patients passive in this process must feel like victims. But I had to fight for my diagnosis, I had to prod and nag the doctors to act; indeed, I had to tell them where to look. I did not receive a "verdict"; I wrenched a diagnosis from reluctant physicians. This was, for me, a victory of sorts, for treatment could not begin until the diagnosis was obtained. Of course, I was not happy to have a cancer, but I was relieved that it was finally named and located. Treatment was thus a positive event, like a reward for my effort.

I called my friends to tell them the news, and heard

in their voices the same odd mixture of feelings I had: sadness that the condition existed, but relief that it had been located and treatment could now proceed. Thus far I had not told my father anything. I hesitated to tell him over the telephone—he was eighty-six years old and very fond of me—and I was unable to drive out to Suffolk County to tell him personally. I called my sister, who lives near him. She knew of my problem with my voice and was not surprised to hear that I had cancer. I asked her to visit my father and give him the bad news. My sister has serious health problems, having only one functioning kidney, and for over a decade has been warned that she may need dialysis or a transplant. She has avoided both by faithfully (and uncomplainingly) adhering to a low-protein diet. Although she rarely mentions it, everyone in the family knows of her condition.

She drove to my father's house one summer afternoon. Isabel always invites our father to *her* house, so he recognized this as an extraordinary event. He received her solemnly. She said she had to tell him something. They sat down, and he spoke first.

"Isabel, you don't even need to ask," he said. "Of course you can have one of my kidneys."

I do not now remember much beyond dread and being dazed, but during the month of June I sometimes jotted down notes about my feelings. These notes reveal great tumult. I was full of grief at losing my life and about leaving my children; I was also in a permanent state of silent terror. I imagine such emotions are ordinary, even universal. But if dying was my great anxiety, it was not my only one.

I was concerned about the fate of my book *The War Against Women*. I had had many interviews, and there was considerable interest in me personally (some of it hostile, as has been the case since *The Women's Room* was published), but almost no reviews had appeared. Even my scholarly book on James Joyce, published in 1977, before *The Women's Room,* had received over a dozen reviews; my novels usually received an inch-high pile of them, and *Beyond Power,* a scholarly analytical study, had been covered well. But *The War Against Women* had received only five reviews, all hostile. The *Newsday* reviewer (a woman) called the book "malignant"—a strange description of a book that is essentially a compilation of facts. The shocking facts are accurately reported; they are distressing, but they make the book essential reading. Indeed, it helped bring to widespread attention facts about the genital mutilation of women, selective abortion of female fetuses, starvation of female babies, and domestic abuse worldwide, subjects that have since been given considerable scrutiny in the *New York Times* and other widely read journals. But the book itself was either ignored or— dare I use the word?—censored.

I say "censored" because in early May I received an anonymous letter from a book reviewer in Britain, saying he or she had been assigned the book and, thinking it was important, written a good review. The review had been returned with instructions on how to attack the book. The reviewer, fearing the loss of her/his job, did the dirty work but felt like a coward, and wrote to tell me about it.

This letter brought home to me how successful the media drive (which has since become even more marked) to censor feminist and democratic ideas had been. Instead of trying to fight or adapt feminism to corporate purposes (as they did in the 1970s and 1980s), male-controlled institutions were now ignoring it, blotting it out. At present, 1998, feminist voices are rarely heard in any medium—print, television, or radio. The few women who are promoted in the media are those who have proved their fidelity to male institutions. The same thing is true of democratic thinkers, called left-wing thinkers these right-wing days. We are told the media are left-wing; but I cannot recall the last time I heard any true leftist voice on television. As the powers that be have shifted to the extreme right, people in the bland middle have been renamed leftists.

This situation, as I became aware of it, weighed me down. I felt that not only was I dying, but everything I had worked for my life long, everything I believed in, was dying too. I sputtered to my friends that I'd been born during the Depression and was going to die in one—a shorthand way of expressing the sorrow I felt about what was happening throughout the country as it was manipulated into a culture that exalts greed and condemns poor and working-class people to greater hardship.

I had for some years seen my life as blessed because it paralleled a magnificent period in American history. I grew up among the poor; poverty and ignorance are not abstract terms to me. As a child, I was familiar with oppression; I saw every day how poor people—and their children—were treated by the world, how women were treated by men, and I had a glancing experience of bigotry against blacks and Jews. But gradually, over the years, many oppressions had been lightened. Assistance was given to poor people so that children were no longer taken from their mothers and incarcerated in orphanages (as my widowed grandmother's were, breaking her heart). Work programs like the WPA and the CCC helped take the edge off the Depression. After decades of struggle, labor unions won the right to exist and strike; following World War II, they became legitimate forums (however exclusive and corrupt). And then, in the sixties, like dawn rising, the civil rights movement began, forcing passage of humane and just social laws. And finally my sun rose too: feminists were able to utilize recent civil rights laws and create a new dialogue, a new language of justice. In the past twenty years, this wave of decency and fairness began to include people of various sexual orientations. My country had begun to forge a world more people could breathe in. These events made me proud to be an American and optimistic about the future of the human race.

Now, sick and probably dying, I watched the entire structure being shattered by greed and mendacity. A President who is still revered broke the air traffic controllers' union, undermining the already demoralized labor movement; he adopted economic policies that enriched even more the top ten percent of the population and led to an extraordinary situation—hordes of homeless people sleeping on freezing streets in every major city in the country. So common has this sight become that we no longer remember it did not always bruise our eyes. The Presidents who followed lazily let the new right-wing thrust—which, I am convinced, arose because of television coverage of the 1968 Democratic Convention, focusing on women, people in wheelchairs, and blacks—continue. The humane experiment had lasted only as long as my puny lifetime.

All these elements combined to create a negative force, a downward-pulling energy. Late at night, in bed, I would sigh, thinking I would not mind leaving this world. It would be a relief to die and no longer feel the corrosive rage aroused by injustice. I was drawn toward death, toward rest, the end of pain, the silencing of a consciousness more sorrowful than pleasant.

This feeling became more powerful later, when I was sicker. But at this point, I could let myself down into this despair and fury as if it were a cold lake, and emerge from it without struggle. I was sustained by my children—Jamie and Rob and his Barbara—and my friends, especially Charlotte Sheedy, the coven, and Barbara Greenberg. It was a shock to me, who had always lived in proud independence, unwilling but also unable to ask for help, to discover how much I needed them: their company, their sweet words, their concerned expressions.

When I was first diagnosed, Charlotte sent me a dozen or so books on cancer, most by megalomaniacal doctors who imply (even as they deny) that they have magical powers to cure cancer. They describe miraculous cures, attributing them to their patients but emphasizing their own openness and understanding direction. I believed in the cures, but not in the doctors. Some books were written by patients who claimed to have cured themselves of cancer without medical treatment. I believed they had good luck. I did not believe people could just decide to cure themselves.

Now that we knew what kind of cancer I had, Charlotte checked with her medical contacts and sent me xeroxed reports on esophageal cancer from medical journals. These professional essays utterly lacked the optimism of the books: dealing only with nonmetastasized esophageal cancer, they reported that treated with strong chemotherapy combined with intense radiation, one of five people survived for five years. Most died within a year. The odds were not great even if the cancer had not metastasized: mine had, and widely, forming tumors outside the esophagus and in two lymph nodes.

Someone else sent me an article from, I believe, an old *New York Times*. It described Susan Sontag's courageous handling of a breast cancer that, when she developed it, was considered terminal. She went to Paris for a severe treatment no American hospital of the time—decades earlier—was willing to risk. I do not now recall whether it involved radiation as well as chemotherapy, but it made Sontag very ill, and it saved her life. That, I thought, was what I wanted to happen to me. But even as I wished it, I knew I was thinking wishfully.

Being a lung specialist, Dr. Strong could not handle my case, alas, but he arranged for me to see an oncologist in the gastrointestinal service. The night before my appointment, Barbara Greenberg flew down from

Boston. I thought she was coming just from affection, which touched me; I did not suspect any other motivation. She had called regularly, and I had kept her up on my condition, but unlike my other friends, she knew I was doomed. She was married to a surgeon who frequently treated cancer and knew that no one survived metastasized esophageal cancer. Barbara came because she wanted to be with me when I saw the doctor who would preside over my dying, and to hold my hand after I heard the news.

The night she arrived, we went out for dinner, Barbara and I and the coven. We ate at Jezebel's, owned by an African-American woman, who has draped the restaurant with antique lace and linens and who serves a luscious Midtown version of soul food. Over dinner, we held a coven meeting, complete with eagle feathers, light-up plastic wand, crystals, and incantations. The other diners paid us not the slightest heed; as far as we noticed, not a single head turned. New York is indeed wonderful.

The next day, Barbara G., Rob, and Jamie trooped with me into the fourth-floor clinic at Sloan-Kettering. The designers of this hospital took pains to make it attractive and comfortable, even in its private areas. Nevertheless, entering it never fails to upset me, because the first-floor lobby is always crowded. An unending stream of people—cancer patients and the family or friends of cancer patients—continually stream through its pleasant corridors: old people in wheelchairs, lovely men and women in their thirties, youngsters with bald heads, babies in their mothers' arms; just looking around can make you weep. I am old enough that for me the word "cancer" is equivalent to a death sentence; I had not kept up with the fact that this is no longer the case. For instance, my nurses assured me that most babies with cancer are cured.

In time, I got in the habit of not looking at people, so as to keep myself calm. Unlike most hospitals, S-K has attractive, comfortable waiting rooms, and its halls are filled with art. For initiates (patients and their visitors), there is a large room at roof level with comfortable couches, a piano, a pool table, worktables and materials for arts and crafts, and access to a garden. Familiar with hospitals as I have become, I judge them by waiting and emergency rooms as well as by their doctors and nurses. A hospital must deal not just with patients but with long-suffering families and friends. And these spaces are far better at Sloan-Kettering than at St. Luke's–Roosevelt or Mount Sinai, the other New York City hospitals I know. The emergency room at St. Luke's is truly shocking, crowded and shabby, especially given its pretentious new lobby, a huge empty space designed to intimidate. Mount Sinai is shocking because its lobby, too, is, like the building itself (whose architect aspired to assert himself so forcefully over the city that he ruined the East Side skyline), pretentious and overbearing, while its actual working spaces—operating, waiting, and X-ray rooms—are cramped, ugly, and uncomfortable.

But on this day, July 23, 1992, I was not aware of any of this; I was shocked into silence by the host of people on every floor, waiting, waiting, all caught in the same epidemic as I.

Sloan-Kettering is a research hospital; each department is devoted to a particular system of the body and has its own staff of physicians, called "attendings." The highest-ranking doctors, they take monthly turns supervising patient care. The gastrointestinal service had five attendings, each "on duty" one month out of five. (Before I was finished, a sixth doctor joined the service.) Each month, one attending was responsible for morning rounds (in which he was followed by a group of younger physicians, still learning), visits to all the patients being treated by the department. At the end of his stretch, that doctor was freed to do research for the next four months. I think all attendings see outpatients two mornings a week; but the system may have changed somewhat since I was there. The young doctors assist the attendings, not only following them on rounds but helping in the research projects, and they gain status from the association with eminence. I have never seen more craven servility than some of these assistants exhibited. I blamed not the youngsters but the arrogant creatures they served. The assistants who dared to talk to me on their own were the pleasantest doctors in the hospital. Humanity had not yet been beaten out of them. But judging from their elders, it would be.

There are many other ranks of doctors at S-K; an entire set works long hours, staffing the hospital at night and on weekends and holidays. Perhaps they are called residents: I am not sure of their formal title. Some older doctors in practice elsewhere seemed to have S-K privileges; I saw them only in Urgent Care (the ER), tending patients who came in with emergencies. Many appeared to be surgeons who practiced in New Jersey or Long Island.

The oncologist I was assigned was not arrogant. He treated his assistant (a warm young woman I would never see again, and missed) kindly and with respect. But he had some characteristics that made him less than an ideal doctor. He was extremely negative. This characteristic took the aspect of dourness or depression, which is understandable in a field in which most patients die (he told me once that his department receives eleven thousand new patients every year, and of those, over ten thousand die). Still, this trait is not especially helpful to patients. Part of his problem could have been his youth. He may not have been as young in years as he looked, but I'd guess he was emotionally immature. Utterly self-involved, and as innocent about this as a child, he had the boyish brightness of a kid in the back of the classroom waving his arm, hoping to be called on so he can recite the lesson faster and more accurately than anybody else. He still saw life as a matter of winning and losing, and he'd probably never failed at anything in his life. Knowledgeable medically and (I am sure) well-intentioned, he could not extend himself outside himself, and so could not connect with patients. He was most likable when he was accompanied by a nurse. At his best working with warm, giving women, he relaxed with them, and they liked him. The nurses' affection suggested to me that he was a good sort (nurses absolutely know whether doctors are medically good and whether they are decent human beings). Their ease with him humanized him to patients, while the nurses gave them human comfort.

He had a difficult job: we were strangers, and he had to tell me I was going to be dead in a year. His solution to this challenge was to speak in an expressionless voice with an expressionless face. He told me I had terminal cancer, that there was no hope for cure or remission, that I was not to think of that. What they could do for me was—they hoped—to shrink the cancer and keep me comfortable. I had a year; for six months of it, they would give me chemotherapy and radiation *if* my kidney function allowed it and *if* I could tolerate the side effects, which could include nausea, hearing loss, loss of sensation in fingers and toes, and extreme fatigue, among other things. If I wondered why I should have treatment when my chances were so bad, there was always a small percentage who did well, and it was important that I think I'd be among them.

What was he saying? Hope, but not too much? Hope, but don't expect a cure? What was I to hope for, then? He emphasized that mental attitude was crucial to anything they did. I spoke up, assuring him that I had strong powers of concentration and that I wanted to hope. . . . But he wasn't listening; he was talking over me. There was no hope for a cure, he said, but they were not trying just to keep me alive in the hospital; they wanted more for me. I couldn't understand what more they could be aiming for, if cure was impossible. I said my swallowing had become easier over the last few days and that I attributed it to my visualization and the coven ceremonies. I also was taking a series of herbal cures and vitamins suggested by friends.

Keep on visualizing, he said, but stop taking herbal medicines and teas and confusing vitamins. Eagle feathers? he wondered vaguely. . . . Chemotherapy would start at the beginning of August. Then he was gone, without a goodbye or a handshake.

I heard what the man said. I understood it. I cried uncontrollably for a long time, with Barbara stroking my back and murmuring sadly, my children hovering silently in the next room, where they had gone while he examined me. It took me a long time to calm down. Eventually, I suggested we look for someplace to have lunch; I was not hungry, but surely they were. We found an Ottomanelli's, and they ate as I stared at the pizza I had ordered. We talked, searching for cheer, as people will.

I don't recall the conversation. But I know that by the time we left the restaurant, I had silently summoned up the conclusions of the medical articles on esophageal cancer that I had read and twisted them to my purposes. One in five people treated with extreme measures survive nonmetastasized esophageal cancer for five years. I decided that the figures applied to me too (despite my metastases): Sloan-Kettering used the extreme measures required. Although none of the oncologists I had met had offered me real hope and most were negative about my chances, I decided I had one chance out of five. I simply made it up.

By the time I got home that afternoon, I had utterly obliterated the word "terminal" from my memory. I never used it in describing my illness to people, and indeed, when doctors I encountered a year or two later acted astonished at meeting someone who had survived esophageal cancer, I did not understand their shock. I had managed to forget totally that my cancer had been terminal; indeed, I had never absorbed the fact that *no one survives metastasized esophageal cancer.* I canceled this fact for myself and for everyone I spoke to. In fierce blind insistence, I decided I had a chance to survive and would count on that. I might as well be part of the one as part of the other four, I told everyone, deeding them all my willful delusion. Within a couple of days, I had changed the figure to one out of four. By then, I had also repressed any sense that I was deluding myself.

This was strange, because I am and have been all my life a person who demands the truth, no matter how unpleasant it may be. I speak it and want to hear it spoken, even at the risk of being confrontational. I have contempt for wishful thinking and comforting illusions, and I despise people who are too timorous to face hard truths. Yet here I was, lying to myself and everyone else.

In fact, hope makes the ordeal of cancer treatment a little more bearable; it provides a basis for feeling a bit of cheer each day. No one who is diagnosed as having cancer fails to be aware that death may be imminent, is indeed more probable than survival; people expect to die even if their doctors offer hope: few cancer patients are overly optimistic, no matter how macho their talk. I remember how suspicious and pessimistic Sibyl Claiborne had looked as she reported her doctor's positive diagnosis. But my doctors were not positive. I suppose doctors deny hope because they do not want to be accused of offering false hope (or sued for it, perhaps), but I think they should refrain from smashing what hope a patient may stubbornly cling to.

Throughout my treatment for cancer, I not only

maintained false hope but denied the reality I had briefly been aware of, the terminal nature of my disease. At no time was I unaware that I would probably die within the year—I had revised my will even before I saw the new oncologist. My mind refused to budge very far, to entertain thoughts of the future beyond a few hours thence. Yet at the same time I felt insistently that I had a chance to live. In this strange state, which may be familiar to others who have suffered a life-threatening illness, contradictory feelings and facts hang together in an easy harmony, like pleasingly dissonant chords in a melancholy music. Either outcome—life or death—seems possible and, after a short time, acceptable.

I had also made a living will and delivered it to my attorney. Having given the subject considerable thought, I knew exactly how I felt about extreme medical treatment. Ever since I turned fifty, I had had conversations with two close friends who were also tough-minded women, Charlotte and Barbara, about the disposition of our bodies should we fall ill in the future. All three of us had read horror stories about people hooked up to respirators or other machines and kept alive artificially for months or years. Indeed, my own mother had had an aneurysm, come to after surgery and stood up, then immediately keeled over in a coma, in which she lingered on a respirator, and with tubes in various parts of her body, for over a month. In that time, she blew up horribly because her kidneys were not functioning properly; I would look at her puffed-up body and weep, knowing how she would have hated being seen like that. And nothing helped. After five weeks, she died.

Charlotte, Barbara, and I all felt the same way about such endings: we did not want them. I knew, knew absolutely, that I did not want to be hooked up to machines, did not want to be kept alive artificially, did not want to suffer the indignity of tubes in my veins, blowing up to twice my size, lying like a lump in a bed, while technicians and coldhearted doctors peered down at me, a piece of meat in a butcher's window. I was a strong supporter of Dr. Kevorkian and of the Hemlock Society, believing that one's end should be in one's own hands. I would do much to avoid humiliation, as I knew Charlotte would. The two of us made a pact that if either of us needed help in ending her life, the other would provide the means. I asked Barbara for such help as well, although we made no mutual pact.

My living will stipulated that almost no intervention was acceptable. If I was not going to recover, I wanted no tubes, no special measures, no machines. I told my children about the will, and where it was, and what it said. But I also told them that my mother, who had dreaded humiliation above all things, nevertheless would not have wanted to be removed from the machines keeping her alive. Though hating her state, she would have clung to life as long as she could. I explained to the kids that I did not want measures taken if there was no hope, but I wanted to hold on to life if there was. Still, I was fairly sure that extreme measures would not be necessary: I felt certain I would never have to suffer such things.

Despite my facade of equilibrium, I was dreading chemotherapy; the first week of August loomed. But my psyche kept playing strange tricks, elevating me to heights of serenity or bliss directly opposite to the depths of my terror. The week before I was to enter the hospital, happiness blossomed like a drop of water on watercolor paint, beautifully spreading and staining the surface of the time.

Early in the last week of July, a friend called and asked if she could come over for a drink. She was a woman I was fond of but not close to, mainly because she was not given to intimacy. We had appeared together on scholarly panels and television discussions, read each other's books, and had dinner together a few times a year. I enjoyed her wit and intelligence. But her call surprised me: she rarely initiated our meetings. Ironically, she often complained that she had no friends, while others complained that she never reached out to anyone. She had never asked to visit me.

She came at teatime on a Wednesday. I poured us drinks and we sat in my study. She said she knew I was very sick. She did not use the word "terminal," or mention death, but conveyed that she knew what I was facing. She knew, she said, that we were not close, we did not speak about our feelings. But then, who did? It was not *comme il faut* for people to talk about feelings. Consequently, people fail to say important things to each other before it is too late. She had seen this happen several times, and she did not want it to happen to us. She wanted to tell me now, while I was alive, that she loved me.

I imagined that professing loving friendship might be difficult for her. So I was especially grateful for her words, for her courage in uttering them and her generosity in making the effort. And that she felt loving toward me pleased me. I cared about her as well, I said. Her act was one of the more moving events of this period, and I will never forget it.

The next day, Gloria went with me to see my oncologist, and she interrogated him as if she were supervising my case. I enjoyed this, since I could not supervise it myself. In certain areas, I have a poor memory, or none at all. My vision is subject to this amnesia: I have often tried to memorize the shapes of leaves, so I can recognize trees, but my eye refuses to retain such information. Whereas if I hear a chord or melody or a line of poetry once, I remember its sound and rhythms without trying. I am amnesiac about figures and scientific facts. I knew I would never remember the details of my case and that Gloria would. She has helped many people with severe medical problems and remembers the specifics, the doctors' names, the treatments used. And for the next months, she supervised my case, even calling the doctor in charge of the gastrointestinal department over the head of my oncologist to ask how I was faring.

That night, the coven met again. At the time, I accepted that these were regular meetings, but looking at my calendar now, I realize how extraordinary an effort my friends made to keep my spirits up throughout this period. That I didn't perceive this then shows how deep my daze was. I went through the motions of living—talking, laughing, eating, moving about—but all the while my psyche was intently pulling leaves off a clover: life, death, life, death, life, death. Though in an isolating stupor, I was not alone. My friends seized me back, embraced me.

Esther came to the meeting with a notarized document invoking on my behalf the powers of her rabbinical ancestors, Aryeh Judah Leib, d. 1770, and Jacob Joseph Ha-Kohen, d. 1782, which descend to the tenth generation, down to Esther Masserman Broner; and of her ancestor the Tsadika, the Sainted One, the great-grandmother who comes in dreams and touches the afflicted, healing them. Gloria brought a beaded leather bag filled with sweet-smelling herbs—mainly sage, I think—which she had been given after suffering through a sweat lodge ceremony held partially on my behalf. Carol brought Zuni fetishes, little silver bears symbolizing strength, one for each of us. Strung on black silk, the fetishes made lovely necklaces, which, my friends said, they would wear whenever I was in the hospital. I was overwhelmed: child of a mother who provided thoughtful and sensitive foresight but not emotional support (requests for it aroused furious scorn), I wept at the thought that when I was frightened or in pain, they would be with me.

Barbara McKechnie, my unofficial daughter-in-law (she and Rob have been together for over ten years), found relaxation tapes to help me visualize. She bought boji stones, which the kids and I spent an afternoon concentrating on, trying to feel vibrations. Giggling with embarrassment or grimacing superciliously, we tried to place faith in what we knew was superstition yet wanted to believe. In time, with tremendous concentration (or self-delusion), I managed to feel some vibrations from the stones. I never achieved it again. Other people—acquaintances, strangers who had read my books and somehow knew I was sick—sent me gifts through the mail or through friends. I was inundated with crystals, sacred stones and rocks, necklaces and pins.

Rob bought me a juicer and made me drinks designed to build up my immune system. He would include carrot, apple, celery, kale, beets, or whatever, which I dutifully (and slowly) swallowed. He and Barbara kept after me, would not allow me to ignore their hideous doses of Nile-green goop.

The kids drove me to the Berkshires every weekend they were free. I was happiest, felt most hopeful, there. One weekend in late July, Rob and Barbara had invited some friends but did not tell me about it. Sunday afternoon, they seemed a bit distracted, especially Barbara. Only the next day did I figure out that she had not been sure they were coming and beyond that was worried about my reaction to them: she had invited people who had recovered from cancer, hoping they would ease my fears.

The guests were Roz and Fred Stein. Roz was a classmate of Barbara's at Hunter; her husband, Fred, a former navy pilot, now worked for the FAA. Roz and Fred had met at a cancer therapy group. Fred, who had had testicular cancer, considered himself cured. He was lively and humorous and passionate about his work. Roz, whose breast cancer was more problematic (she had developed it as a young woman, and it had already recurred), was courageously going on with life, studying French with Barbara, going for a degree. She was witty but driven by dread.

I would grow fond of this couple, who in the next years became good friends of Rob and Barbara, but the effect of their first visit was not what Barbara had intended. Roz, a thin, nervous, handsome woman, had only recently stopped treatment; her cancer was again in remission, but she was obsessed with the idea that it would recur. She had gone on a macrobiotic diet, to which, though it was difficult to manage and not very palatable, she was committed. She could speak of little else but possible recurrence. At one point, I said, "You're okay now, aren't you? The cancer is gone?"

"Yes," she said.

"Well, why don't you try to concentrate on that for a while?" I suggested. "Think about being better, take pleasure in it, try to relax."

She looked surprised, as if offered a path she didn't know existed.

"Yeah," she agreed. "I should."

But she went on talking about recurrence as if it were inevitable. Some might say—I might have thought it myself—that by harping on recurrence she might provoke it: the anxiety alone could cause it, or so it seems to superstitious minds (and when it comes to cancer, most of us are superstitious). But knowing what I know now, I could as easily say that she knew her fate, her body knew, that she was trying to come to terms with a devastating knowledge.

Listening to her, I was growing more and more uncomfortable and wishing I could leave the room, when she announced suddenly, "Well, if it does come back, at least I have my port!"

I asked her what she was talking about.

"My port," she repeated, fingering a spot on her neck. "They put a port in my neck. It's a kind of permanent hole into a vein. They close it with plastic until they need it. Then they won't have problems hooking up the IV the next time; they won't be sticking and sticking me, unable to find a good vein. You know, your veins get blown after a while."

I fled. I thought I was going to be ill. Such things were beyond my comprehension, and I wanted them to remain that way. I didn't want to know about ports and IVs and blown veins. To calm my stomach and head, I had to go outdoors. I put my head on my hands, tried to erase from my mind everything I'd just heard.

Two years later, Roz died, as the dear soul had been trying to tell us she would.

The last weekend in July, Rob drove me to the Berkshires with Barbara and Jamie, for a last quiet time together, a time for eating well, relaxing, and enjoying the end of summer, the last time before I would be made sick—how sick we couldn't guess. Carrying lunch and choosing a short walk from our hiking guidebook, we went for a hike in the mountains. But we got lost, and hours later were still wandering around in the Berkshire hills, until we stumbled onto a road marked "Appalachian Trail" and Jamie's sense of direction kicked in. I lay down on the grass, unable to move, while Rob trotted on his long legs back to where Jamie swore (correctly) we had left the car. We are not a family that denies our emotions or represses conflict. We flare up at each other and fight, sometimes fiercely. But on this day, no one got upset or pissy; we laughed at ourselves and our plight; and by the end of the weekend, I felt as contented as someone in my situation could feel.

1992

AUGUST

On Tuesday, August 4, I entered Sloan-Kettering for my first course of chemotherapy. S-K has a smooth, efficient admission procedure, managed by cheerful, high-spirited black women who take vital signs, give EKGs, and arrange for X rays where needed. They welcome you as if to a luxury spa rather than a grotesque and painful new chapter of life, your first formal step toward death. They are friendly and agreeable but, at the same time, profoundly disengaged; such pleasant, disinterested guardians might admit you to a euthanasia salon or to the country club gates of heaven or hell.

It can be quicker, but usually takes an hour or more to get checked in and sent upstairs; once you are there, it can be quicker but sometimes takes hours before the nurse assigned to you finds you, takes another complete history, and gets you settled in a bed. On my first stay, I was sent to the eleventh floor, where the nurses are specially trained in administering chemotherapy. Whatever floor you are on, however, the S-K nurses are spectacular—superefficient, knowledgeable, warm, compassionate, and so agreeable that they make you believe they care about *you*. In this, they differ hugely from the nurses in other city hospitals I have sampled, especially St. Luke's–Roosevelt, where the nurses and aides are often surly and resentful, or Bellevue, where (I hear) they are downright ugly. Nurses in country hospitals, like Fairview in the Berkshires, can be pleasant and even fun, but they are not as superlatively trained as S-K nurses.

Chemotherapy patients stay in hospital for six days on average at each visit, and they return every month for six months or more, so the nurses often get to know them. A nurse who tended me during my first visit stopped in frequently during later stays to say hello. Assigned elsewhere on the floor, she would make a special trip. "I heard you were back and hoped for a free minute so I could run down and say hello," she would say, smiling. Some nurses remembered details of former stays; one asked, "Did you get your teddy bear?" (On a previous visit, Carol had brought me a white teddy bear, insisting that I learn how to cuddle it. I loved the bear but could not manage the cuddle, and because it did not fit into my bag, I forgot the bear when I left. My nurse tagged it and held it for me.) I have heard that S-K is reducing its nursing staff. I hope this is not true. The nurses are the only institutional factor that makes hospitalization and chemotherapy endurable; they provided my only pleasant memories of the hospital.

I entered with determined good spirits, feeling a certain triumph in having wrested a diagnosis from apathetic doctors and being able to start treatment. In addition, I had had to pass a test of kidney function in order to receive cisplatin. Hearing this of course immediately raised cisplatin to wonder drug status in my mind: I actively *wanted* to receive it and was elated when I inched through the required numbers.

Still, I had heard enough over the years about chemotherapy and radiation to know that they could be horrible experiences. A friend from past years, Barbara, a young doctor married to Barry, whom I'd known as a Harvard graduate student, had felt ill for some time before she drew her blood and sent it to the lab of the hospital where she worked. Though past childhood—she had an M.D., after all—she had childhood leukemia. Her long siege of treatment carried her several times to the edge of death, including a near-fatal coma, and caused her immeasurable suffering. She came through it with Barry's loving care, but said afterward that if the leukemia recurred, she would not undergo the torture of treatment again. Elated as he was at her recovery (and she is still healthy and vivacious), Barry condemned chemotherapy as barbaric, like the treatment of mental patients in the eighteenth century. I had never forgotten this.

Another friend's mother had had breast cancer and, while going through chemotherapy, needed a transfusion. New York Hospital gave her contaminated blood; she developed AIDS and died five years later.

These were just two of the horrible anecdotes I knew, part of the collection we all carry around. They contributed to the subconscious content of my dread.

Rob went with me when I entered S-K. Although chemotherapy would not start until the next day, the nurses immediately hooked an IV line into a vein in my arm and began to hydrate me in preparation for the toxins—fluorouracil, or 5FU, and cisplatin, commonly called platinum. On my second day in the hospital, Wednesday, August 5, the nurses began the fluorouracil. Two nurses are required to administer chemotherapy—they check each step aloud together, one reading out the doctor's order, the other reading out the words on the medicine bag, checking name, strength, dosage, and other factors. They hang plastic bags of chemicals and saline solution on the arms of a tall, skinny metal pole mounted on wheeled legs. Lines from the bags are fed into a blue box, which controls the rate at which the liquids are pumped and coordinates their passage. A line from the box runs into the IV needle in your vein.

I watched the nurses like a bird of prey, ready to swoop down on them. As politely as I could, I questioned them. Smiling, carefully using a nonaggressive tone, trying to tell them that I doubted them less than I feared death, I mentioned the two women in the newspapers the previous month, killed by mistaken chemotherapy doses at their hospitals. So—just checking—did they have the right chemical? the right dosage? They did not become defensive in the least, but—well-trained or humane—answered all my questions kindly, saying they understood. Over the years to come, many nurses would tell me they had had cancer themselves.

The 5FU had no immediate effect on me, and my dread relaxed a bit. Not until the third day did they administer the cisplatin, following the same steps as before. (Cisplatin is hard on kidneys. My oncologist had said the process might improve my kidney function by thoroughly hydrating them, but this proved to be wishful thinking.) As the platinum entered my bloodstream, I sat alert, like someone being executed, waiting to feel the lethal charge: I had the sense that cisplatin was deadly and expected to feel its toxicity. But over the next days, I felt little except some twinges of nausea, which were quickly controlled by a new drug, Zofran. I began to relax. This business was not as bad as I had been led to think, I decided. So far it was nearly painless.

The patient is connected to the IV pole at all times, day and night, for six days or more; any clothing worn on the upper body has to be donned or removed around these tubes. I loathed wearing the loose, thin hospital gowns, which are humiliating and not very warm. The temperature at S-K is kept low, good for equipment, not patients. So after my first hospitalization, I designed a top with sleeves connected by Velcro strips, not seams, which could easily be donned or removed over the IV lines. My sister took the design to a seamstress, who made me tops from richly colored velours. I wore these throughout my hospitalizations— at least when I was conscious.

The IV pole is hooked up to a large plug in the wall, but the cable reaches far enough for a patient to go to the toilet or sit in a chair; one can disconnect it from the wall for several hours at a time and pull the IV pole down the hall to the kitchen, or take the elevator up to the roof lounge. The day I left, I saw several people, including a very young woman, standing outside the front door of the hospital, hooked up to their blue chemo boxes, smoking cigarettes.

Pleased at my relative well-being, I used the laptop I had bought especially for the hospital to write a few pages of the novel I was determined to finish before I died. But I had an unending stream of guests and so many telephone calls that I got little done. Rob bought me an answering machine to turn on when I wanted to get some sleep or was away from my bed.

A problem I face with every hospitalization is privacy. Private rooms are prohibitively expensive; at the modernized St. Luke's–Roosevelt, for instance, fancy private rooms sit empty on every floor because they are priced so high. (At the time I was there, they cost $500 a day more than semiprivate rooms, which themselves cost around $2,000 a day before charges for medications or treatments. My health plan, Florida Blue Cross/Blue Shield, paid $80 of that.) At S-K, the system was entirely fair and sensible: the price difference was negligible, but private rooms, identical to two-bed rooms, if smaller, were reserved for those getting bone marrow transplants. Only when no such patient needs it is a private room available to others. But I did not object to sharing my *room*; what I minded was *television*.

I craved silence, and I was often blasted by TV all day, and sometimes all night as well—some people *never* turn it off. Even if I complained and a nurse requested that it be turned off, roommates might keep it on while they (but not I) were sleeping. Most people refuse to use earphones. And in these enlightened days, nurses no longer order patients to do anything.

I am not a television hater on principle. Before my illness—and again now—I watch television on evenings when I eat dinner at home alone, and I enjoy a good movie or a drama from the BBC. But I cannot tolerate the intrusiveness of a TV running constantly, as is the case in some homes and ICUs. And for some reason, once I knew I had cancer, television repelled me. I couldn't stand it and never turned it on, at home or in the hospital. During my illness, television felt like an instrument of oppression. My television-watching hospital roommates drove me to spend nights on the short, uncomfortable couches in floor guest lounges (ugly, uncomfortable places to sleep in, even in S-K), or harry the nurses to change my room, or threaten to leave the hospital entirely. The only roommate worse than a constant TV watcher is someone with Alzheimer's who shouts or sings the same song or phrases for twenty-four hours a day—literally. I roomed with such a woman at St. Luke's–Roosevelt, where men so disordered often held forth noisily in the hall outside my room all day long. However, I encountered no Alzheimer's patients at S-K.

My first roommate during this first course of chemo was a sweet, mild woman who said she could not use earphones to watch television because chemotherapy had damaged her hearing. I didn't know how earphones would impinge on damaged hearing, and I thought then that she was an anomaly. (But hearing *is* usually damaged by chemo.) Luckily, she did not watch constantly, and a doctor offered me the use of the doctors' lounge, a narrow room with a single bed (usually unmade) and a long wooden table surrounded by wooden chairs. I used this room on several occasions but had trouble concentrating there. This is not unusual for me: I have trouble working anywhere but my own space. It was easier for me to write in bed than in the doctors' lounge; maybe beds are interchangeable enough to fool my literary psyche-blockers.

This roommate had had several months of chemotherapy and had severe problems. I wasn't sure whether her cancer was advanced or if her problems resulted from the chemo. I was dismayed—no, *shocked*—to find myself turning away from her and her problems: I disapproved of myself. It has always been a point of pride for me to confront the harsh or unpleasant, refusing to turn away from the ugly or uncomfortable. Yet now I was becoming the kind of person I scorned, someone who preferred smug complacency and comfort to acknowledging the pain in the world. But I didn't want to know what was happening to this woman; I didn't know what to expect from chemo, and she made me fear for myself. She seemed to be alone in the world except for a loving sister, who visited her faithfully every day and took her home after a couple of days.

The beautiful young woman who arrived next did not watch television at all—a blessing for me, not her:

she was simply too depressed. Only twenty-nine, she had developed breast cancer a few years before and had a mastectomy, but now the cancer had recurred and was in her spine, liver, and stomach. She often called the nurses, to whisper that she was in pain and ask for medication. Suspecting that she was dying, I asked the nurses, who murmured that she was very sick. One hinted that she didn't have long. Since nurses are honor bound not to discuss their patients, the fact that they answered me indicated how distressed they were. They were very kind to her, but she, locked in terror and sorrow and pain, was hardly aware of them (or me).

I was so appalled by her family's treatment of her that when they visited, I tried to concentrate on writing or reading so as not to overhear. But it was impossible not to eavesdrop on her life to some degree—she was only a few feet away from me. The first night, her husband, a policeman, brought his cop friends to visit her. They were sweet and hearty but uncomfortable, and they left quickly. Her husband walked out with them, returning only long afterward.

The man—short, dark, well-built, handsome—spoke little; words were wrenched from him. When they were alone, he was very involved with her, not lovingly but in a power struggle. He kept trying to pin her down, to force her to say definitely if she was really going to make him go for psychotherapy or divorce him when she got home, as she had apparently threatened. She equivocated. I couldn't tell if she feared to say what she wanted or if she didn't know; perhaps she suspected she would not be going home. But she was clearly trying to pressure him.

After a while, the details filled in. The night she asked him to take her back to the hospital, he beat her up. She wanted him to express remorse, but he never did; he wanted to shrug it off, forget it. He was profoundly involved with his wife, but as a service: he was concerned not with her, but with his fate, his comfort. Though he did not want to go for therapy, he also did not want her to leave him. His wife was extremely important to him, but only as a means to his well-being, not in herself. It did not seem to have dawned on him that she would soon be leaving him permanently. He had to have been totally locked in himself not to recognize that she was dying.

She had two sisters, or foster sisters, who visited frequently and probably thought they were doing good. But they were busily, noisily cheerful—a common response to illness. People mean well and do not see how distancing insistent cheeriness is, how it denies another's reality, denies a sick person the space or right to be sick and in pain. She tolerated or ignored them, asking often for her mother, who was really her foster mother. The sisters made excuses for the woman's absence. It was a long trip for her, one said; the other scolded the patient for expecting so much. One day she burst into tears, crying that she needed her mother, wanted her. And finally, she appeared, a tired middle-aged woman, indifferent and uninterested, even annoyed, talking constantly about how busy and overworked she was, especially now that she was tending the sick woman's son. The young woman was reduced to whining for a little love, but she did not get it. And when one day the husband brought in the little boy, a child of about eight, she barely spoke to him, completing the hellish family dynamic.

A doctor visited her a few times and vaguely discussed possible treatments, including a bone marrow transplant. She placed her hope in the transplant, mentioning it to each visitor at every visit. But he did not arrange for treatment; he dillydallied, as my doctors had until I prodded them. I conjectured that her doctor was reluctant to subject her to so painful a treatment when she had little chance of surviving it, that he was really waiting for her to die. But maybe I was making this all up. In any case, she was still in that bed when I left the hospital. I never saw her again.

No one in her world seemed strong enough to console the poor soul; she had to face death alone. Observing her with profound sympathy and identification—I, too, had felt myself an unloved child (but now I was loved!)—I considered my situation nowhere near as sad. I could face death with some equanimity: I was sixty-one years old and had had a rich, satisfying life, if also one of intense suffering. But I believed that some of my suffering was caused by my own intensity, my fierceness and volatility; I had made everything hard for myself. Yet I had also, slowly and stumblingly, created the life I wanted. I had known what I wanted when I was ten, known it with a clarity and passion that I felt could not and would not be thwarted, although I had gone off track and for nearly two decades lived a false life.

But I never forgot my path, never completely deserted it. I craved knowledge of all sorts—of literature, philosophy, history, art, music, *life*. I wanted to feel easy with that knowledge, and write out of it and my principles and taste. I hoped to be published but never expected to make much money from my writing (just enough to live on, I dreamed, not knowing then how rare even that was). I wanted to travel all over the world, to have all sorts of sexual experiences with all sorts of people, and to have cultured sophisticates for friends. I imagined an elite who lived on a higher cultural plane than others, whose conversation was lofty, who had innate good taste, grace, and dignity. It never occurred to me to ask also that they be decent human beings. I wanted a town house on Manhattan's East Side, with a black front door and a brass door knocker. And I had realized all my desires to some degree. Still, I had not had enough; I wanted more; I could never have enough. I had not yet been to Japan, or to South America. . . .

Oscar Wilde said that there were two tragedies: not getting what you want, or getting it, which was worse. But I am happy I got what I wanted, despite the ironic character of fulfillment.

At fifteen, I had no desire for husband or children. I got them, as it were, by default, like any good girl of the forties. Yet now my children were my greatest satisfaction, my greatest pleasure, my greatest love. And they were grown. I grieved over not seeing or touching them again, not knowing what would happen to them, but not over leaving them helpless and vulnerable in a world in which no one would ever love them as I did— like my poor neighbor. If I lived longer, about all I could give them was my pleasure in their existence. It was ironic, I thought, that two things I never thought to want when I was young—children and good friends—were two of the three essential elements in my life, the third being my work. The unwished for, the unexpected, turned out to be the greatest blessing. Pure luck.

Pondering again the randomness of fate and the sadness of that poor woman's lot, I ached to talk to her, to help her in some way—but how? Who did I think I was, that I could help? No one could help a woman who had never been loved and was now dying. Like my own mother, she was beyond consolation. Still, I knew that it sometimes helped simply to listen to people—I've done a huge amount of listening in my life. So I did try several times to start a conversation. But I could not penetrate the isolation her sorrow cast around her.

On the other hand, if I was in some ways more fortunate, in other ways we were the same, she and I. Death is death, we both faced it (she a little more closely) alone, as everyone does. I, too, longed for my mother to come and comfort me, yet I knew that alive, she would have been unlikely to offer me comfort. My mother was steeped in the suffering of her childhood; she saw any illness or pain of mine as an act of willful aggression against her, causing her, who felt she had already suffered more than any other human being on earth, even more agony. Sliding into the bitter self-pity that (it seems) mothers can always provoke, I decided it was just as well my mother was dead, so she did not have to deal with my illness and I did not have to clutter up my heart with rage against her. Still, night after night, lying there unable to sleep, I tried to reach her, calling on her silently wherever she was. I could not feel her: she had turned her face away from me.

Another bad thing about all hospitals is the food, which is not only tasteless but poor in quality. Cooking for so massive a number of people may inevitably cause tastelessness, but I do not understand why hospitals buy unhealthful foods. The importance of nourishment to health is a matter of common knowledge, so why do trained dietitians continue to buy Jell-O, plastic-like ice creams and desserts, cheap, gluey white bread, the castoffs of the vegetable markets, tasteless, tough cuts of meat? Then they cook the food into oblivion, removing any nourishment it might have had. This seems to be true in all hospitals.

As it turned out, for me it did not matter how good or bad the food was: I could not eat. The kids and my friends brought me good soups from home or a restaurant, casseroles I could heat in the hospital microwave, lovely pastries, whatever I said I felt I could eat. Carol trekked across the city to a bakery that sold madeleines (which I could and did eat); Jamie prepared a casserole of macaroni and cheese the way I had made it for them when they were children. Rob was always searching out a soup or pastry I could get down. But I could not eat much, and as time went on, I could not eat at all. The smell of the chemicals on that floor has never left my body's memory, and since my chemo treatments, I have never been able to eat in a hospital, any hospital.

Chemotherapy has profound and lasting negative psychological effects on many people. I feel upset each time I pass Memorial Sloan-Kettering Hospital on York Avenue. Some people become nauseated passing the hospital where they were treated. My oncologist told me about a patient who became nauseated each time he laid eyes on his oncologist. One summer, on holiday, walking along a Paris street, he experienced sudden extreme nausea. Turning to his wife in bewilderment, he asked why he should feel this here now. Then, glancing back down the street, he recognized a man who had passed him a few seconds earlier, whom he had not noted then—his oncologist.

On Monday, August 10, a week after entering, I was released from the hospital. My assistant, Isabelle de Cordier, fetched me and carried home my laptop and the bags of stuff I had somehow accumulated in six days. Go home, live normally, the doctors said. I was high: I had survived chemotherapy without serious damage! I had been through it and survived. I was home. I went upstairs and showered (hospital showers are ugly, uncomfortable, and unpleasant) and put on fresh clothes.

But once the euphoria of being home had passed, I did not feel well. I tried to work. I had written a little over a chapter during my hospital stay; I had another five chapters to write to finish the first draft of the book. But I could not write; nothing came. My children came to make dinner for me that evening and gathered around me when they saw how weak I was. They scolded: I was not drinking enough, I was dehydrated, I wasn't eating. But I couldn't drink or eat: I could barely swallow, I didn't know why. Was I having a psychological reaction, after six days of not eating? With the kids hovering beside me, I sat at the kitchen table, concentrating, trying to get water down. But it did not want to go. After another day of this, I called my oncologist, who told me to come in to Urgent Care. From there, on Thursday, I was sent back to the hospital.

Urgent Care, S-K's emergency ward, open only to S-K patients, was to become familiar to me over the next months, as I suffered from one or another "side effect." The day of my diagnosis, my oncologist had mentioned some side effects of chemo, and new chemo patients get an information packet containing a statement about patient rights and printed cards listing the possible side effects of each chemical—a perfunctory way of meeting doctors' obligations. But nothing can prepare you for what is to come. The simple phrases—mouth sores, mild nausea, diarrhea, loss of hearing, neuropathy, possible hair loss, temporary decrease in blood cell counts, and others—cannot convey the physical reality of what happens to your body. Nor does anyone inform you that these effects are often permanent. If you live, you live damaged.

Still, what would we do if they told us the horrible truth? That cancer treatments damage the body less only than cancer itself, and that much of the damage is lasting, every oncologist knows. Simply to treat cancer means they must violate the primary tenet of their code: First, do no harm. But the harm varies hugely from patient to patient and with kinds of cancer. Radiation of the breast, say, affects the body less severely than radiation of the esophagus (which hits the spine and heart). I think the age of the patient is also pertinent: judging by my friends and acquaintances (among whom breast cancer is epidemic), treatment of breast cancer is nowadays tremendously successful in older women (and men), less so in younger ones.

S-K's Urgent Care is not like emergency rooms in other hospitals: because it is limited to S-K patients, it is smaller and less chaotic than most ERs. No one can enter it from the street. Patients are admitted and cared for with dispatch, as a rule. But like other emergency rooms, it offers little privacy.

I have spent time in five different ERs but have never seen one that in the least resembled the TV version in degree of privacy and space or in noisily catastrophic events. I have never heard doors exploding open or seen a team of people frantically pushing in a trolley. When serious emergencies do occur, every care is taken to keep them quiet. And the governing ethos of the ER is not, as in television presentations, a matter of dominance—the brilliant doctor performing brilliantly, the noisy rebel upsetting the routine, the urgency of new cases mustering the entire staff. ERs are quiet and feel calm, if busy, whatever the reality. The main characteristics of ER nurses and aides are cooperation and amiability. The doctors vary in degree of indifference and disinterest (although in a small hospital like Fairview, the ER doctors tend to be lovely). Moreover, there are usually only one or two doctors in an ER, which is mainly peopled by nurses and orderlies.

In Mount Sinai's ER, when I was there, the central figure was a black male nurse who was especially solicitous of his patients and seemingly connected in a friendly way to every other nurse and orderly in the room. Beds were lined up against two walls, facing each other, with a walkway about a bed's length wide between them. I was in that ER for hours, and because it was so crowded, I lost my cubicle whenever I was sent to X-ray or other labs. I was left in the walkway between the beds then, and I could see the activity at both rows of bedsides. Curtains were rarely drawn. At one point, a guard moved through the room, quietly asking all guests to leave. Later, I asked the nurse why that had been done. Were there visiting hours in the ER? I had never seen that before. No, he replied, but they had had an extremely urgent case at the other end of the room and needed to keep all extraneous people out, needed to concentrate on the patient. The room was not that large, and I had been there during the time this case was treated, yet I had not been aware of it.

At S-K, each patient, when summoned, is placed in a bed in a narrow cubicle formed by pink curtains. You can always hear (and, when the curtains are left open, see) what is going on with the three or four patients near you. The S-K hospital hierarchy is naked in this miniature world. Any white male you see (you see few) is a doctor (I never saw a female doctor in Urgent Care); any white female is a nurse. Black females are rare at S-K (I encountered only one black nurse in my visits there), but black men are common, walking in and out collecting wastes and delivering supplies.

The nurses in S-K's Urgent Care are even more spectacular than the chemotherapy nurses. They are not permitted to diagnose, but of course they do, silently; like nurses in other emergency wards, they know who needs care quickly and do what they are permitted to do. They perform the many required procedures with swift efficiency and intelligence. You may wait a long time for a doctor, but you feel safe once you are in the nurses' hands.

One or two of the doctors I saw in Urgent Care during the six months I used it were pleasant people who treated patients like human beings, but most were peremptory and dismissive. I also saw doctors who were not S-K attendings but men with private practices elsewhere and privileges at S-K, who cared only for their own patients. They made the S-K doctors look like models of knowledge and professionalism. Almost all of these visiting doctors were horrifying to watch and listen to, loud, bullying, arrogant, and impatient. I found this unforgivable, considering that their patients were not only sick but frightened by whatever crisis had brought them in.

On my first visit, I was lying next to a heavyset man, older than I, who also had esophageal cancer. His doctor, a surgeon from New Jersey, had operated on him and he was left in horrible condition. He could swallow food, but it did not remain in his stomach. The loud-voiced, bullying doctor asked him questions, but his answers were vague. He kept saying, "My wife knows, my wife keeps track." He was vague even about his medications. Finally, the doctor ordered the wife to come in and give him the information he needed. Deeply involved with her husband's treatment, she had everything at the tip of her tongue: when he had pain and how long it had lasted, what he had eaten and when, and when it came back up. She knew about his bowel movements and urination, his medications and sleep patterns. The doctor declared that another operation was called for. The patient and his wife accepted this submissively.

Another time, a handsome man in his early forties lay sleeping in the end bed. A beautiful woman sat beside him silently, watching. She often bent forward to lean over him—perhaps he had moved, or an eyelid had fluttered. During the many hours I spent in the ward that day, no doctor approached them, and the devoted woman never moved. No words were necessary to demonstrate her love. She still stands in my memory as a kind of symbol, patience on a monument.

One afternoon, a nurse silently pushed in a young man in a wheelchair, with a basin in his lap. The nurses scurried to ready a bed for him, but for a few minutes he sat visible in the center of the room. No one saw him but Rob and me (the other patients' curtains had all been drawn). I drew my breath in sharply at the sight of him: he was skeletally thin and as white as the albino boy in my first-grade class. He was bald—probably from chemotherapy—and his large, egg-shaped head was sickeningly white. As I watched, he opened his mouth and bent over the basin, spilling perhaps a pint of blood into a basin already half full of blood. He was young, in his twenties, probably, and dying. He was one of the most terrible sights I'd ever seen; his suffering—which I could not begin to fathom—was palpable, although he spoke no word and made no sound, past complaint.

In my many visits to Urgent Care, all the patients around me were men; I don't know why. But I was glad for the exposure, because the difference between them and the women with whom I shared rooms upstairs was striking: men usually had women to care for them, whereas few of my roommates had men visit them, and none had a man taking care of her. Women were visited mainly by other women; women were the caretakers for patients of both sexes, although I never saw a woman take care of another woman in the detailed, careful way the wife of the man with esophageal cancer cared for him. Except for the boy in the wheelchair, all the men I saw in Urgent Care were accompanied by wives and sometimes sisters and daughters as well. An elderly Chinese man came with an entourage of women. When he was about to be discharged, two nurses patiently tried to instruct the women on how to take care of him once they got home. Through considerable language difficulty, they told her they could not keep him from getting up to go to the toilet—he was probably a proud man. One nurse talked with them for a long time, attempting to dredge up ways to salve his pride while keeping him off his feet.

A few of my roommates had husbands, but none took responsibility for their wives like my friend Barry. One man came every night with his dinner steaming and fragrant in a paper bag, and sat there eating, gazing at his wife. I was touched by this; I thought: How sweet; he's used to eating with her and probably can't bear eating without her. I went on thinking this and smiling at the man each time he entered the room, until the night her weak, weary voice protested:

"Lou, did you have to bring chili in here? You know it makes me sick to smell it. All these spicy dishes make me sick." He said nothing; he finished eating. I wondered if his dinners made her sick every night. After they left, I thought: I wouldn't be surprised. Because on the day she was to depart, she was smiling and happy. By the time he arrived, she had put on her street clothes and came out of the bathroom wearing a big smile and a brownish-blond wig.

"What do you think?" she asked, her eyes bright, eager for a compliment.

"Looks like hell," he growled.

So much for sweetness, I thought. With someone like that around you, your chances of recovering were very low. I blessed myself again that a former lover who had left me had done so long enough ago that I was over it by the time I got sick. I knew that if we had still been together, I would have been deserted as soon as I was diagnosed, and that that would have crushed me, perhaps enough to affect my prognosis.

One roommate had a grown son who had been away—in Europe, I think—and had not seen her since before she fell ill. Now he came every afternoon to play cards and chat with her; he took an interest in her medical treatment and stayed to speak to the doctors and ask them questions. I, too, had a devoted son. Neither of these sons took responsibility for their mother's care (I did not need this degree of help and probably would not have allowed it), but both were deeply involved and interested in all its details. I also knew—presciently—that if I did need help, my son would give it. At Urgent Care, I was a lucky woman. My children or friends or both sat outside waiting for me, and when they were allowed in, they sat by my side, silent, waiting, still. Rob always sat with me for hours, holding my hand. A lovely doctor in Urgent Care came upon us this way one day and was startled.

On my first visit to Urgent Care, I was diagnosed with thrush, a fungal disease that sometimes occurs when many white cells are killed off. It sounded trivial to me, but the doctors considered it serious and said I had to be hospitalized. It was serious, they said, because it indicates a low white cell count and it was blocking my internal organs—at least my throat, which was why I could not swallow. (In subsequent months, I was given a medication before and after chemotherapy, to prevent thrush from developing.) After a long wait, they admitted me to the hospital, though not to the eleventh floor, which had no free beds.

The nurses said it was not uncommon for patients to return to the hospital mid-month. But when that occurs, treatment is not a relatively easy one-week-in, three-weeks-out. As it turned out, I spent about three weeks in, one week out, almost every month. When first diagnosed, I had another dread besides that of dying. As I went from doctor to doctor, I saw hundreds of people in hospital waiting rooms, lab waiting rooms, doctors' waiting rooms. They sat for hours, patient and silent, waiting, waiting. I was one of them, but never patient. Restless, impatient, I harried receptionists, clerks, whoever; I protested three-hour waits. (By the following year, I was shouting at doctors who made the mistake of appearing in their office when there was a long wait.) I felt that these patiently waiting people had stepped in the elephant dung. (There is a saying in academia about working in a low-status

college: If you once step in the elephant dung, you will
track it around behind you forever afterward; you can
never get rid of it.)

The elephant dung this time was the condition of
being sick: not suffering from *a* sickness, an occa-
sional bout, but having a chronic condition of illness.
For such people, illness was a way of life. Their days
were centered around appointments with one doctor
or another, picking up a new prescription and keeping records of side effects, trying the new herbal
tonic a friend had recommended. Husbands and wives
together made the sickness of one (or both) the focus of their lives. Sitting for hours in a waiting room
was a common part of this kind of life, something to
be endured tolerantly, something expected. If you
were a cancer patient, the hospital and the doctors
became your life, constituted your entire life, circum-
scribed all the conditions of your life. Beyond weeping that this was what one's life had become, what
was one to do?

My adamant determination that this not happen to
me contributed to my bad temper at being kept waiting,
but besides impatience, I suffered from a piercing need
to escape. As a child, when faced with threats from
other children, or disapproval from an elder, I would
raise my head and eyebrows in the most supercilious
manner I could manage and try to sail above it (suc-
cessfully most of the time, I must admit). So now I
raised my head and set my mouth and vowed they
would not get me, I would not become a professional
patient, I would remain a human being, a thinker and

writer who was temporarily ill. But in the end, there is
no escape.

The day after I was readmitted to the hospital, I developed what are called mouth sores. Like many chemo
patients, I would develop them every month. This
sounds innocuous, but it is horrible. The chemicals in
your blood kill all fast-growing tissues in the body.
Besides cancer cells, they destroy the soft tissue in the
mouth, throat, intestine, and bowel. Cuts in the inner
wall of the mouth, the gums, and the tongue hurt
when you try to eat or even talk. Two or three times a
day, a nurse comes around and sprays your mouth with
something—boric acid?—that calms the pulsing heat
of the cuts. But the relief is short-lived. The sores
lasted about two weeks, ruining most of my (supposed) out-of-hospital time. A seemingly minor problem, mouth sores are agonizing.

But the nadir of this second hospital stay concerned
television. I was again fortunate in my roommate, who
willingly used earphones when she watched TV and
did not watch it constantly. I knew that the Republican
National Convention was occurring that week in
Houston (though I did not watch TV, I had the *New
York Times* delivered every day, and Isabelle brought me
The Nation) and that Pat Buchanan was to give the
keynote address. Fervently hoping that my roommate
would not want to watch it, I was relieved when she fell
asleep early that evening. But I was not to escape—a
man down the hall was determined to watch it and
force everyone on the corridor to hear it. He tuned his

set so loud that it blasted the hall. I begged the nurse to ask him to turn it down; she grimaced, saying other people, too, were complaining, but the man absolutely refused to reduce the volume.

For me, Buchanan's speech was symbolic. In my vulnerable state, I had no defense against it; it fit right in with my mood of despair. The speaker's words, his tone, epitomized everything about my country and the world that made me receptive to death, made me feel on occasion no regret about leaving this world. So do impersonal events collude in our lives and our death.

I had expected to remain in hospital for a couple of days, but they kept me for eleven, until Sunday, August 23. In tearful frustration, I realized that in only seven days I had to return, for another course of chemo. Seeing my dismay, the kids offered to take me to the country for the week. We drove up to the Berkshires on the day I was released, and I breathed more easily, as I always do there. But I was weak and enervated from being so long in bed without eating. There were no hikes in the mountains this time; I had only the luxury of lying on a chaise on my screened porch with the kids, surrounded by the fragrant garden, watching hummingbirds fight in the bee balm and the delphiniums, the orioles, the finches, robins, hawks, blue jays, and sparrows play.

The morning after we arrived, I was combing my hair in front of my bathroom mirror, and a huge clump fell out into my hand. In wonder, I touched the back of my head, and another huge clump appeared in my hand.

Losing my hair was the one side effect I had antici-
pated. I had shrugged it off. So what, I thought. I told
my friends, I can handle that; it's nothing. So little do
we know ourselves! For when it happened, I burst into
tears; I found it horrible. I felt like a leper, as if my
limbs were shriveling and dropping off. Within a few
days I was completely bald. I stared at myself in sorrow. In my youth, women would stop me on the street
to ask what shampoo I used to get such shiny hair. We
were too poor to buy shampoo, and my mother had us
use Ivory Flakes, but I never confessed that to anyone.
Now I realized I had taken pride in my hair, it had been
a source of vanity, even though it had lost its sheen
long ago. I walked around the house bald, but I covered my head when I went into public.

One magical thing happened during the month. It was
so remarkable that I recorded it in my laptop journal.
The night I was readmitted to the hospital, I was restless, unable to sleep. Words from a Rilke poem kept
running through my head: words spoken in an afterlife
by a little boy who has died, to his living parents. In the
translation I know (Randall Jarrell's, I think), he says:
"Here everyone is like a just-poured drink / But the
ones who drink us I still haven't yet seen." The thought
was transformed in my mind into a repetitive "Here
everyone is just a body broken," and I consciously
appended, "and the ones who treat us see us that way."
In the hospital, brokenness had become the dominant
factor of every patient's existence.

I found this idea comforting, which was odd, since I
had spent most of my life high-handedly ignoring my

body, demanding that it do what I willed it to. Yet it was somehow a relief to be reduced to mere body, as if I were a baby again, not responsible for anything, my body cared for and watched over and monitored. This was the full human-merely-human state; I could not pretend to more, hope for more. I watched skinny-legged men speed down the corridor pushing their IV poles, their hospital robes flapping behind them, their skin whiter than if they were already dead. A permanent if not constant feature of the hospital was the sound of women weeping. I would often hear a woman crying softly in a room down the hall, and a nurse would pass my door, her eyes wet.

I could not relax that night. At last, unthinking, unaware of what I was doing, I told myself to have pleasant dreams—as my mother did every night of my childhood as I went to bed. "Good night, Marilyn, pleasant dreams," I said to myself as she always said, and at that moment I felt her presence. She *did* care that I was sick, she *had* noticed. She had turned her attention away from herself and toward me, for a brief time, at least. I could sense her horror at my broken body and my pain, and she smoothed my brow with her hand, something she had done once in life, when I came out of surgery. I asked her to make me feel better and to stay with me until I was well. Then I was able to sleep.

She never appeared to me again, but it was all right. I knew she knew and cared.

1992

SEPTEMBER

A week later, on the last day of August, I returned to S-K for my second course of chemo. This time, I was given a private room, and I managed to get more writing done. I was surprised one day by a visit from my sister, Isabel, and my niece, Cary, who live on Long Island. I had earlier signed up for a small event for female cancer patients—a demonstration of makeup; the flyer promised that experts would teach us how to tie scarves to create an attractive head covering. I would have canceled, but Isabel and Cary were interested in going with me.

Twenty or so women attended the demonstration, held in the penthouse waiting room. One of them I had seen frequently on my various wheelchair journeys around the hospital—to the X-ray department, the audio department (for a hearing test), and other test sites. Each time I saw her, I imagined that she was on the verge of dying. Always in a wheelchair, she was pushed not by an orderly, as I was, but by a woman I took to be her daughter. Several men often accompanied them, the woman's sons, perhaps, or her brothers (none seemed to relate to her as a husband). All looked to be from a foreign culture. The woman looked old but could have been younger than I; she seemed disconnected. I imagined she did not speak English. What most struck me about her was her color, a bluish-grayish yellow, the cyanotic color of a corpse. I was sympathetic to her and her family, because she looked so sick and so out of it; but the whole family seemed dazed, never looking directly at anyone. I invented a scenario in which all had come here from some alien place—Albania or Uzbekistan—and were living in terror in this foreign land while their mother received medical care.

The makeup demonstration was probably financed by a group of cosmetic companies, two or three of which had contributed most of the large bagful of cosmetics we were each given. Two young women did the work. Judging from their spiels, they were saleswomen. A young man seemed to be in charge, but he said and did little. The women were young, shallow, and criminally ignorant: they had been trained only to spot and deal with troublemakers (like me). They had no training whatever in the effects of cancer on the human body.

We patients, in various stages of illness, sat around a long rectangular table. I sat across from the cyanotic woman, whom I was surprised to see at something like this. Maybe she wasn't as sick as I imagined. But she did look and act like a corpse, her face livid, expressionless, and she unspeaking. Yet she participated, slowly and confusedly trying to follow directions. She must have understood English to some degree, but she needed help in following the directions. She never spoke or looked at the other patients or the women instructing us, or at me, who, directly opposite her, looked at her frequently. Indeed, most of the women focused their eyes fixedly on their mirrors, as if they dreaded meeting another person's gaze. I wondered whether the problem was that they could not bear finding their images reflected in another's eyes; isolated with their mirrors, perhaps they could idealize themselves. Most women know how to do that, if only for its calming effects.

The instructors' superficiality and fake sophistication would have irritated me even if I'd been well, but when a skinny, highly made-up young woman announced dramatically that "Eyebrows are *in* this year, ladies!" I was appalled. Such a statement was ludicrous in any case, but many around that table had lost their eyebrows along with their hair. I said nothing, but glared in disapproval. Both instructors immediately approached and began to lavish attention on me, hardly what I wanted. They also attended to the other trouble spot—the woman across from me. She was a problem not because she said or did anything, or looked angry, as I did, but because she was so out of things. Purring patronizingly, they removed the cosmetics from her bag and showed her what was what. She never visually or verbally acknowledged them, but she did seem pleased, patting her face ineptly with cream or blusher or eye shadow. One instructor finally took over and helped her apply foundation, eye make-up, blusher, lipstick. During the hour and a half of the demonstration, she never uttered a word.

My indifferent manner continued to cause anxiety in the instructors. I did not care. Doing the job they did, they should have known more about the condition of the people they were dealing with, should have been more sensitive to it even if no one had bothered to inform them beforehand. But in truth, none of the patients seemed in the least upset by their tactlessness— except me.

In the end, after sitting through the entire miserable performance, I asked for a demonstration of head coverings and was told they knew nothing about them. I had sat through this grotesquerie for nothing! The only good thing to come out of the session was the bag of makeup I was later able to distribute to Cary and Isabel, Barbara and Jamie, and any other visitor who wanted it.

Again, the drugs caused me no immediate pain, but when the six days were up, the doctors refused to discharge me. They said my white count was too low. They asked me about bowel movements. When I told them I had had none for five days, they acted as if this was an extremely serious problem—yet they offered me no help with it; I started to worry and drank the prune juice Jamie had brought me. Two days later, the doctors let me go home. (Throughout chemotherapy, I suffered from excretory problems, moving regularly and swiftly between diarrhea and severe constipation, with no modulation between states. Drinking prune juice was touchy, because the constipation might be on the verge of becoming diarrhea, which prune juice exacerbated.)

Home again on Monday, September 7, Labor Day, I poured bath oil in the tub, tuned the radio to WNCN (still a classical music station in those days), and luxuriated. Rob and Barbara came and made me a pot of delicious chicken soup, which I was able to eat. But a few hours later, I had a painful gastric attack, took several doses of Mylanta over a period of hours, and suffered explosions of diarrhea. I woke from sleep, choking and coughing up blood. Calling the emergency number, I was told to phone again the next day. I continued to bring up blood, and that afternoon the doctors told me to come in to Urgent Care.

Again, Rob took me to the hospital. The Urgent Care doctor—not the sweet one this time—acted as if something very serious had occurred but would not tell me what. He put an oxygen tube in my nose, at which I wept behind the pink curtains, drawn after they left. This was it, I thought, the beginning of helplessness and indignity, the most horrid part of dying.

I lay there for hours, listening to conversations between doctors and their patients, struck once more by behavior I had noticed in my roommates. Most people do not question their doctors but simply accept what they say. Doctors propose horrendous things, and people just nod. This shocked me, since my automatic response when a doctor ordered something, even something relatively innocuous—a bone scan, an

X ray, a CT scan—was to ask why it was necessary and what information it would provide. Once informed, I rarely challenged an order.

When a doctor said to a man in the next bed, "I'm going to have to operate again—we'll try to put a tube between your esophagus and your stomach. Let's get your wife in here again to set up a date," the man simply said, "Yes, Doctor." In other hospitals, I heard doctors tell patients they would have to remove a kidney, or perform some painful procedure. But even the woman told that her kidney needed to be removed did not question the need, did not ask, Why do you need to do this, what will you discover? Will this help the pain? Will this help heal me? Will I die if you don't do it? She never asked, How will I fare with one kidney?

Patients simply nod. Men and women are equally passive in this situation, and so pervasive is this behavior that doctors unfamiliar with me often bristled when I questioned the purpose of a test or procedure, as if I were trying to balk or challenge them. They were used to passive obedience.

I do not think this passivity makes an important difference in the quality of medical care, because most of us (including me) are too ignorant to know if the explanation we are given makes sense or is true. (Why do I need a fourth chest X ray in four days? To make sure the pneumonia is completely gone. Oh, okay. You already took blood twice today, why again? Oh, a different test. Okay.) But it does contribute to the arrogance and high-handedness of doctors. Unquestioned, they proceed like hollow gods. The great majority of my doctors, male and female, were informative, respectful, and kind. I can count on the fingers of one hand—well, two hands, but I've dealt with literally hundreds of doctors in the past five years—doctors who attended me even briefly who were surly or nasty or indifferent or arrogant. I found incompetence to be even rarer. Ignorance, however, is everywhere, and bless the doctor who admits it, because *all doctors are ignorant.*

But my reputation preceded me in my hospital stays; most of my doctors knew I was a writer, knew I had a certain repute: I was treated as a person of status. The situation for people without status was very different. With each new stay in a hospital, whatever hospital, I was again shocked by some doctor attending a roommate, or by one occasionally assigned temporarily, *very* briefly, to me.

On this day, the Urgent Care doctors were aloof and uncommunicative, verging on rude. On this day, as on many other days, I said nothing. I was sent upstairs, to what I discovered was the "heart" floor (there were heart monitors at each bed). It was dark by the time I got upstairs. A large staff of young, inexperienced doctors (who were often as brusque as their betters) was always on duty at night and on weekends. Two young doctors hooked me up to a machine that was new to me. These guys were sweet and humorous. When I asked what they were doing, they said pleasantly that they were hooking me up to a heart monitor. Why? I asked. They said I had had a heart attack. "What?" I cried. I asked them if they had compared today's EKG with the one from my admission earlier in the month. S-K keeps tons of records (my S-K file is literally almost five feet high now), but doctors rarely read old records, and more often than not, the pertinent document is missing. They had not found my earlier EKG.

I informed them that I had not had a heart attack. (In those days, I thought I knew what a heart attack was like.) I said it had felt more like an ulcer attack to me. (When, in 1994, I *did* have a heart attack, I also thought it was an ulcer attack. So much for my astuteness. In my defense, I did not argue with the diagnosis the second time.) They stared at me, then at each other—with a wild surmise (precisely). It could be that, they agreed in some excitement. That might explain things, they said. What things? Well, the fact that my heart was beating strongly and steadily. They gave me an ulcer medication, and when, two days later, I demanded to be sent home, they let me go. I still take the medication they gave me then.

The day I left the hospital, mouth sores had developed again. In August, they had appeared eleven days after the chemo started, and lasted thirteen days. In September, they began on the tenth day after the start of chemo, but began to ease ten days later. That I recorded these sores on my calendar this way suggests how large they loomed in my life, how painful they were, and how I dreaded them.

People continued to be assiduous in their attentions to me. Perhaps it was from duty, but they blessedly made it feel like affection. Carol visited me almost every day during my September hospital stay, often late at night, after visiting hours were over. S-K is relaxed about visiting hours, and no one ever tried to stop her. Carol was anchoring or reporting on the eleven o'clock news on NBC in those days and could not get away before midnight. She would show up at twelve-thirty, and the nursing staff would go into a frenzy. Female voices shrieked in joy: "Carol Jenkins! Carol Jenkins!" I became a minor celebrity in several New York hospitals because of her visits, for Carol is one of the most beloved women in the city, as anyone will discover who walks with her down city streets.

Rob, Barbara, and Jamie came constantly. Barbara was so attentive and loving that my nurses thought I had two daughters. Esther and Charlotte, Linsey Abrams and Ann Volks, were also faithful visitors. Every day I was in the hospital, two or three people came to see me, and when I got home, someone stayed with me every night. They did this because I asked them to; it was a measure of my desperation that I did so. It was incredibly hard for me to ask anyone to do something for me, but during this period I did. By now, my white count sometimes dipped quite low after chemo, and I often ran a fever. When this happened, I would call Urgent Care and usually be told to come in. I was afraid that I might have to go there in the middle of the night, and I shrank from having to go alone. My old independent self was not even a memory. The new me dreaded trying to find a cab and riding across town alone, then lying in Urgent Care with no one outside waiting to hear how I was. But neither did I want to call people late at night, especially Rob, who lived in Staten Island and had a long journey into the city. That he always came without complaint did not mitigate my unhappiness.

The word went out among New York's feminists, and several women, like Catherine Stimpson (not a close friend, just a generous-hearted one), called to offer themselves for night duty. Remembering how feminist historians had rallied around the historian Joan Kelly and her husband during her protracted siege of illness, I felt grateful on entirely new grounds for this great movement and its wonderful members. I recalled how nineteenth-century women always gathered like ministering angels to a sick one in their midst.

Barbara and Rob stayed with me on Friday night and again prepared a lovely dinner. But I could barely eat, and that night I had the first in a series of nightmares about poisoned environments: Rob and Barbara and I were in a gambling casino (an apt metaphor for the hospital, I decided) that was sinking into toxic mud that surrounded it. Throughout the rest of the dream I made frantic efforts to escape from this treacherous building with my children. I awoke, then drifted into a heavy, poisoned sleep. Yet I woke in the morning feeling refreshed and energetic, free of pain except for my poor cut-up mouth. Just feeling good was bliss after days of weakness, probably from my low white count. I sat in my bed drinking tea and gazing out at Central Park and a gorgeous sunny day, and a happiness more intense than any I had felt when I was healthy poured over my body like sunshine. An old friend, Herb Weiss, had called earlier in the week, offering to take me for a drive in "the country." I decided to phone him that day.

I was eager to see where Herb's "country" was: I wondered if he knew some secret back road to a rural paradise near New York City. Herb took me along the west coast of the Hudson, on the Palisades Parkway. And indeed, it was country. That Saturday drive was a treat. Still somewhat weak, I just sat back and relaxed, letting the light and the green of the trees and grass in the soft September day play on my eyes, my face. That drive affected me deeply. Before falling ill, I took great pleasure in walking city streets, observing the movements of life everywhere around me. But my illness had estranged me from the world. Each time I left the hospital, I would stare from the cab at familiar streets, busy as always with people following their usual course, but the sight did not cheer me. People, noise, activity—nothing dislodged my sense of disconnection, of being ill; nothing erased the hundreds of sick and dying people still visible behind my eyes. The concerns of normal people were not my concerns: my concerns were suffering and dying. When I got home I would lie on a couch in my study and read or listen to music, trying to blot out bad memories.

But in the rural atmosphere of Palisades Park, people were hiking. Herb and I agreed that since they were walking for the sheer pleasure of it, they were probably European. Americans, especially New Yorkers, exercise for goals other than pleasure—they run or bike, often against a stopwatch, working up an aerobic sweat. The hikers *looked* European—they wore dresses or trousers and hats, not sweats or spandex—and they proceeded in couples or small groups in a smiling, leisurely way along paths resembling the mountain paths they were probably used to. For just so do people walk in the Alps outside Geneva, walk and, when they pass you, bob their heads, murmuring, "M'sieur, 'dame." (It is true, they are stiffer-mannered there.) Herb parked the car, and we got out and walked a little, not far; my muscles were weak. But while we walked, I felt part of the world again—not a patient, but a woman taking pleasure walking in the mountains on a friend's arm. I, too, was part of the greenness and the soft day; whatever my eventual fate, I was alive now. I felt like a person, not a sick body.

During the next nights, though, I had more toxic dreams. Several centered on a friend who was going through a disastrous time. Her entire life had collapsed: while she was suffering from the inflammation of a long-standing psychological problem resulting from childhood victimization, the political situation in her country changed, causing her to lose her job. Her brilliant career vanished; without an income, she had to sell her house and, in the situation, accept a price far below what she had paid for it. In addition, her lover broke up with her. She was far away and I could do nothing to help her, but I was sick with worry for her. She was a frequent figure in my dreams throughout this period.

I was hospitalized for most of the first half of September, but during the second half, I felt fairly strong and free of pain, except for the mouth sores. I was able to stay out of the hospital. I am staggered by the realization that many people work through their chemotherapy. There was no month that I was strong enough to have held down a job with regular hours. The most I was able to do when I felt good was to write; I never even cooked. But my personal regimen included doing two things religiously: visualizing, and seeking pleasure in the moment.

To visualize, I used a tape Barbara M. had brought me; designed for cancer patients, it was narrated by a sweet-voiced man. It took some sifting to find this tape; Barbara and others had brought me several. Listening to them, I discovered that I was supersensitive about speech. I could not bear sharp or flat voices, unmusical voices, or Long Island accents; bad grammar or mispronunciations made me toss a tape out immediately. Militant imagery—frequent references to making war against cancer, attacking it, destroying it— also upset me. So did New Age music. The tape I ended up using had one war image and some New Age music (now, when I hear the pentatonic scale as used in New Age music, I feel literally nauseated), but the accent was cultured, most of the images agreeable, and the man's voice a caress.

I needed the tape; I could not achieve the state I thought necessary without it, mainly because I cannot fully relax without help. And to reach the intense pitch of concentration required for visualization, one has to be fully relaxed (or so I believed). Once you are relaxed, the voice instructs you (first) to visualize your body fighting the cancer (the one military reference) and (second) to see yourself healthy. I could not bear to think in terms of fighting (strange, when I've been such a fighter all my life), because the thing I was supposed to fight was part of myself. So I visualized my white cells surrounding the cancer in an embrace and shrinking it, not in hate but as part of a natural process, transforming the cancer into something benign. Then

I imagined—felt, really, so deeply was I immersed in these visions—a radiant blue light inside my body, emitting magical radiation that cleansed and healed everything it touched. I stayed with this for a long time, longer than the tape directed, and would have preferred to remain even longer, but guides are insistent. Like the audio aids in museums, they deny you any freedom: on to the next picture!

The next step was to see yourself in a place you love and feel good in, healthy and active. I put myself in various spots—a small boat in the Mediterranean, standing beside a man I loved, looking forward to our landing spot in Tunis or Hydra or Alexandria; alone, in Greece, at the temple of Sounion or in Delphi, stooping to drink from the Pierian Spring; or in the old walled city of Jerusalem, where I had had semimystical experiences. But no matter where I imagined myself, I always ended in my Berkshire house, lying on the chaise on my porch, surrounded by the gardens. I would force myself to rise and walk across the lawn to the pool, then step into its charmed, warm water to swim with strength and pleasure. But this part was harder to see.

The tape ended soon after this, and I often fell asleep before it finished. I believed it did not matter if I slept through part of it; I thought it entered my unconscious mind and was just as efficacious. I used this tape twice every day, afternoon and night, at home and during hospital stays.

I actively sought pleasure in every day, a habit I had always believed in but rarely pursued. Even on days when I was weakened by fever or in pain, I would seek some source of satisfaction. When I was in bed, I lux-uriated in the sight of the park from my bed; when I could eat, I would enjoy some delicious food. I was always elated by a stimulating discussion with a friend (something that occurs frequently in my life), when I was strong enough to have one; or a visit from some-one I loved, or listening to music I loved. Rob had bought me a portable CD player to take to the hos-pital; Charlotte had brought me a foot-high box of Mozart CDs, which Carol complemented with an album of Billie Holiday CDs. I was absorbed in the books I read (if not, I did not read them). And some-times a feeling of rapturous well-being would simply rise up and embrace me. I *cultivated* this sensation, something I had not known one could do. But until I became too ill, I had at least one experience of bliss every day.

Linsey Abrams gave me one of the books that en-chanted me that month: Diana Souhami's biography of Gertrude Stein and Alice Toklas, which also sketched the lives of other expatriate women in France in the twenties. Most of them had private means and lived with great style, which is to say they lived for pleasure. Some wealthy women in America did the same—Herb and I had seen the remains of Grecian columns on a platform along the Hudson that once figured in the social world of such a group; and the less affluent Edna St. Vincent Millay built a charming garden at Steepletop, which functioned as a salon.

But Gertrude and Alice were experts at pleasure. Everything they did was directed toward it. They loved to eat well (Alice was a great cook, and when they were in the country, they grew their own vegetables). They loved to talk and listen and entertain, laugh and eat in company. They read and wrote and walked and looked at art and bought it and decorated rooms and drove around the French countryside. Although they were not free from snobbery and the desire to impress, they and the other expatriate women were less concerned with impressing others than with enjoying life. Oh, I know I'm idealizing them, but if you compare their lives to the lives of the fathers who had earned the fortunes they lived on, or the brothers who had the privilege (and pain) of continuing in the fathers' footsteps, the difference between a life lived to gain profit and prestige and a life lived largely for its own sake is clear. Some of these women worked, of course. Stein had to write to earn money; Adrienne Monnier and Sylvia Beach built businesses, but their business was books, which yield more pleasure than profit.

Since the demise of a leisure class (which I do not lament), only a small elite live for pleasure. But nowadays it is not a group accidentally made rich by a forebear, but a self-selected group composed of ordinary people who make a determined choice to move to Vermont or some other rural area and live frugally by distilling maple syrup, or some such thing. They include graduate students on tiny stipends who make their fellowship a private aristocracy, academics who trade wealth for a life immersed in thought or art. I have lived this way since 1968, although I always worked hard and had no money until after *The Women's Room* was published, in 1977. Those of us who choose pleasure without money lack the smashing high style of people of wealth, however. This is a loss, but I could not forget that while these women were striding around being brilliant and glamorous, my grandmother was working in a sweatshop and weeping every night for the children taken from her and put in an orphanage. Yet I hate ruining every image of style and ease by puritanical disapproval.

The next book I read served as a serious corrective to this lovely vision of life. *Death Without Weeping,* by Nancy Scheper-Hughes, describes a town the author calls Bom Jesus, a slum in northeastern Brazil, inhabited by cane cutters recently removed from their land, working wives, and their children. The author, an anthropologist, brought her own children with her on at least one stay in the town. Her motherhood was part of the impetus behind this book, an anatomy of horrible poverty and disease (owing to things like wages too low to feed even one person, much less a family, polluted water, lack of social services), because the author was so horrified at the fact that the mothers of Bom Jesus do not weep when their infants die—as they regularly do.

But what horrified me most in her vivid picture of the lives of these people, what remains with me still, is how their culture succeeded in brainwashing them, even without television. The people are black, and so poor that they are often starving. *But they do not know it!* They have lost touch with their bodies. Observing the Portuguese who lived in the city, they saw tall, straight-limbed, healthy white people. They concluded that their own problems with diseases they called *nervos, gastos,* and *foma* were a consequence of their race. Starving, they went to a *doctor,* who, although he had to know better, gave them prescriptions for tranquilizers! When their infants cried out of hunger, they gave them sugar water laced with tranquilizers. Of course the babies died.

On Tuesday, September 15, Rob and Gloria accompanied me to my oncologist's. I had missed my previous monthly checkup because I was in the hospital. Gloria questioned the doctor far more intelligently than I could have; knowing she had telephoned Dr. Kelson, the head of the gastrointestinal department, some weeks before, he treated her warily. (I had not known about this and was privately delighted. Only recently have I discovered that he informed her the average survival time for patients with esophageal cancer was eighteen months—six months longer than my oncologist said. But never, then or later, did she indicate that she had been told this.) The oncologist directed me to have a CT scan to see if the chemo had shrunk the tumor, and I made an appointment for Thursday. I felt well enough on Saturday to go shopping with Jamie for a wig.

I knew from years earlier, when wigs were fashionable and my hair was long and I spent miserable nights sleeping in curlers, that wigs were hot and itchy. But appearing bald in public embarrassed me—even if privately I rather liked the look. The thing is, people stare. And a woman going out bald seems to be making a political statement, like the singer Sinead O'Connor. But Sinead O'Connor, bald or hirsute, is beautiful and young. If I looked like her—or if I had brown skin, a long neck, and a thin, beautiful face with strong cheek-bones (like my acquaintance Yolande)—I'd happily go bald. As it was, I never went out of the house without a head covering.

I had drawn up a list of wig shops in the area of Fifty-seventh Street but soon discovered that only one specialized in cancer patients—Edith Imre, where I was treated well. The other shops were staffed by glam-orous young women who were horrified by the sight of a bald head and gave me sullen, lackadaisical atten-tion. I chose a plain brown wig that looked natural (and was insulted when people took it for my own hair). Then Jamie and I went to a gallery down the street to see a Lucien Freud show. Since it would turn out to be my last such event for years, I am glad Jamie was willing to accompany me, despite her profound dislike for the artist. I respect my daughter's convic-tions and would normally not have asked her to go to a Freud exhibit.

The next day, Sunday, I had another lovely day in the country. This time, Perry Birnbaum, a pal from college days, picked me up and drove me out to Sag Harbor to visit another college friend, Gloria Beckerman. I hadn't seen Perry in over a year, and we talked volubly, catch-ing up; Gloria served us lunch on a patio overlooking the water. It was a beautiful day, my friends were fun, and we dished—or they did and I listened, pleased that I could chew and swallow even meat and bread (with care), thrilled to be there, under a tree embracing us with shade, the water a deep blue.

On Tuesday, Rob and I went to my oncologist to

hear the results of my CT scan. We waited, as usual, an hour or so, then were ushered into his consulting room. The doctor entered, speaking as if he had already examined the X ray, but clearly he had not. He turned away from us to study it, talking all the while. I, too, was studying the CT scan, but I could not find the tumor. (I knew where it had been.) Still talking about what can be expected from a mere two months of chemotherapy—"a little shrinkage, perhaps, if we are lucky"—the oncologist paused, peered more closely, then announced in a tone of shock, "Your tumor appears to have disappeared."

Because of his tone of voice, I had little reaction to this at first—he sounded appalled by what had happened. Finally, I did some thinking for myself, and joy leaped in my heart. "Does that mean I can have less chemotherapy?" I asked, smiling.

"*No! No!*" he cried angrily. "If anything . . . well, you'll have to go through at least the regular course." He sounded as if he wanted to punish me with an even longer course of treatment. Perhaps he was irritated because his expectations had not been met; the scientific predictability of his work was more important to him than I was. I am sure he did not wish me ill, but I was just one more in a series of dying patients. How dare I confute the statistics? Besides, it would surely grow back. There was no reason for me to be elated: the cancer would recur, and I would still be dead in a year, or a year and a half.

So pervasive and powerful was his negativity about the vanishing tumor that I did not allow my spirits to rise. But I teased him (perhaps I was angry, too). Fingering the beaded leather bag of herbs I wore around my neck (which Gloria had brought me from her last trip to the Cherokee Nation), I said, kidding, "It's the sweat lodge ceremony that did it." He turned swiftly, a little wild-eyed. *"What?"*

I held it out to him. "Smell it," I urged. It was fragrant with sage and other herbs.

Hesitantly, with distaste, he lowered his nose to within six inches of the bag, then moved away. He said nothing and left soon afterward, having reminded me to show up for my next course of chemo on September 29, a week from that day.

Rob and I went out to lunch, giggling and, like the doctor, wild-eyed, but with wild smiles beneath. I did not know how much hope to attach to the disappearance. The doctor had insisted that the cancer would recur; it was expected to recur; he did not want me to get my hopes up. But why should I not? How often did this happen? Wasn't it at least a sign? Rob was so happy that I suddenly realized how depressed he'd been. It was a good development, wasn't it, despite the doctor's behavior?

At home, I immediately telephoned my friends. Charlotte went over the moon: she leaped to the conviction that my cancer was gone forever. I was cured; it was a miracle. Her assurance shocked me. She was so uncompromising, so absolute, she could not even hear me say that the oncologist had almost promised it would return. Her relief made me realize how heavily my illness had weighed on her, what a reprieve it would be for her if I recovered. I did not know until years later how distraught she had in fact been. Charlotte was my agent, had been for sixteen years; but almost from the start we were also friends. She was as close to me as a sister; I loved her deeply. And she seemed to feel the same. Dazed, I had not noticed that during these past three months, Charlotte had been a wreck. She "looked like hell," her more observant friends said; she often went without eating and slept in her clothes; and in this frenzied state, she had run her business, appearing sane and in control.

The coven, overjoyed, planned a celebration dinner for the next night. I said we could have it at my house—I had not hosted one of our dinners in a long time; Gloria had had them all (Esther had a houseful of people living with her, and Carol had moved to Westchester). I called a caterer and ordered a lovely meal.

The next evening, Wednesday, September 23, the waiter arrived early, bearing dinner, and set the table in the dining room. He had forgotten to bring wine, and I had none in the house, so he called his kitchen and asked someone to deliver a couple of bottles. Esther and Carol arrived around seven; we were sitting in the study, eating hors d'oeuvres and sipping drinks, when the boy arrived with the wine.

Suddenly, all the lights in the building went out. The electricity died, which meant that not just the lights, but the stove, the refrigerator, and the elevator were not working. And I was on the twentieth floor. We all crowded onto the front terrace and, looking down, saw fire engines below. The telephone rang (I later discovered that my telephone was the only one working in the building): it was Gloria. She had arrived a little late because she had been working on strategy with Bella Abzug, who was campaigning to fill the seat of a just deceased congressman. The firemen would not let her come up. (She would have had a terrible time walking up forty pitch-black airless staircases—two to a floor.) Actually, she was some blocks away, because there was no phone on my street. She said she would walk back and wait, and perhaps they would get things under control and allow her up.

The waiter was beside himself. He worried, he paced, he called his kitchen. The delivery boy just shrugged. I did not understand why anyone should feel frightened; I felt no fear myself—after all, clearly there was no major fire, and if there were, surely we could be rescued from one of my terraces by helicopter. It would be an adventure! Carol, well-known to all city officials, got on the phone. Calm and gracious, the complete professional, she spoke on and off all evening to a pleasant, patient fire chief. It was only because of Carol that we learned anything that night. No one took responsibility for informing residents; there was no announcement in the building; no one visited the elderly to calm them and make sure they were safe.

There had been a small fire in the laundry room, which was being refurbished. It was quickly extinguished, and the rest of the building was in no danger, but the laundry room contained asbestos titles—in ceiling or floor—and so the EPA had to be called in. Part of the refurbishment was the replacement of these tiles. In fear of asbestos contamination, the firemen kept people out of the building. And indeed, they never let them in. Gloria told us she did not see anyone coming out of the building, either—which did not make much sense. She kept calling, giving us whatever information she picked up from the rescue trucks and the many residents milling around in the streets, even from as far away as Broadway. She called from a phone in front of a McDonald's, where she had gone for coffee, and later from a Chinese restaurant, where she had gone for dinner. We had no dinner: it could not be heated. We filled up on the cold hors d'oeuvres.

In our attempt to distract the poor waiter, Esther discovered that he was an aspiring singer and encouraged him to sing to us, which he did, beautifully. Unfortunately, he was ignorant of the reason for our celebration that night, and he sang about death and graveyards. I asked Esther to stop encouraging him, and he retreated into the dark kitchen, where he sat with his head in his hands, near tears. The stoical delivery boy simply gazed at him, expressionless.

I gathered the chimney candles that were scattered around my house. Being a writer-reader and having endured many electrical storms, I have learned that you can read by candlelight only if the light stays still—which requires a chimney. We lit candles in the kitchen and the study, although the study, where we sat, was already fairly bright, its large window facing Central Park and the rising moon.

We talked late, laughed a great deal, and lamented when Gloria called to say she was giving up and going home. I made sleeping arrangements: there were enough beds (and rooms) for three women and the waiter; the delivery boy could lie on a couch. Out of blankets, I gave him my fur coat to keep him warm. But the waiter was afraid to sleep, and he sat up on another couch in the same room. Esther and I went to bed. But Carol sat up all night long to stand guard over Esther and me, to protect us from anything that threatened. Later, when everything was over, Carol said, "There has to be a force field protecting you. Otherwise, why were you the only person in the building whose phone worked?"

The next morning, Isabelle, my assistant, appeared for work as usual, and no one stopped her, although she had to use the stairs. She responded to my guests' pleas by going all the way downstairs again, fetching coffee for everyone from a restaurant on Broadway, and carrying it back, climbing twenty flights again. Inspired by her example, the waiter and the delivery boy plucked up courage and left. Yura, the caterer, never sent a bill, although I urged her to: none of what had happened was her fault, and she had provided a fine dinner (which went bad, of course, the refrigerator being off). Catastrophes, even minor ones, do tend to illuminate character.

We three of the coven had had a wonderful time, as people often do in crises that are not seriously threatening, and my fellow witches often retell the story of that evening with great gusto. This may be the reason that I never took action against my building, the Ardsley, for its negligence during the crisis. No one ever offered an explanation for the events, and the next morning, during one of poor Isabelle's treks up and down the dark, stifling back staircases, she encountered a bent-over, aged woman peering out of her kitchen door. Quaveringly, she asked what was going on.

Because of the EPA's involvement, the matter took weeks to resolve. There was no electricity, and therefore no way to live in the building, until well into October. I had to call the doormen every day to ask if the electricity had been restored yet: no one took responsibility for informing the residents about that, either. And although I put in a claim, the building's insurance never repaid me for the nights I spent in a hotel. I stayed at the Mayflower for one night, then the kids drove me to the Berkshires for the weekend; on my return, I stayed at Gloria's for a night and the next day, September 29, reentered S-K for my third course of chemotherapy. Released on October 4, I returned to the Mayflower, but was able to go home the next day.

The day after the fire, Isabelle helped me move to the hotel (chosen because it was near my home and garage) with some clothes and my laptop, books and the bag I kept packed for the hospital. I was able to help her: I could still carry things and walk with energy. I felt buoyant, high on my friends' laughter the night before and on my latest CT scan. There was a PEN board meeting that evening, the first of the season, and I made the long trip downtown to attend. I felt confident that attending this meeting would mark the resumption of my old life, that now I would be stronger between hospitalizations.

But it was a sorry meeting for me. A couple of women made nasty cracks about my mousy hair color, not realizing I was wearing a wig. I was incredulous:

did they *want* to hurt my feelings? If so, why? I must be showing vulnerability (something I'd managed for years to avoid); nothing like that had ever happened to me before. I'd heard girls in school talk of other girls' cattiness, and I was familiar with supposed female cattiness from movies and plays, but in my sixty-two years, I had never encountered it firsthand. I didn't understand why they found it necessary to say anything.

Then I saw Sibyl. I was so happy to see her, I rushed toward her. We had not seen each other since February, and she wanted to know how I was—she knew I, too, had cancer; Grace Paley had told her. I told her the chemotherapy had made me quite ill but had also made my tumor disappear, though the doctor promised it would recur. She wished me luck, but her mind was elsewhere. She had been a connected, gracious woman, and she looked at me while we talked, but I sensed she was not seeing me.

And how was *she* feeling? This aroused no greater interest in her. She was all right, she said indifferently. She had gone to a hospital on the Cape for treatment three times a week and had the rest of the time to herself. She'd played tennis all summer. The chemo had not made her sick. I wondered why her treatment and mine were so different, and our responses too.

Sibyl said she felt great bitterness toward her body for inflicting this terrible disease on her. She hated her body for it. And the chemo wasn't working; her tumor had grown and spread. It was in her lymph nodes now.

I knew she must have oat cell cancer, the type that develops in the lungs, which is fast-growing; whereas I had squamous cell cancer, a slower-growing type, found in organ linings. But it was also true that hers had been detected when it was tiny, whereas mine had metastasized widely before it was discovered. Yet mine had vanished, and hers had grown. I did not understand why.

Mine had also been in the lymph nodes, I said.

"Was yours like this?" she asked, taking my hand and laying it on the flesh above her clavicle, where someone as thin as Sibyl would normally have an indentation. Instead there was a hot huge swollen mass. I was appalled and must have shown it.

"Oh. No. I didn't have that. Is it painful?" I asked, trying to hide my dismay.

"No," she said tonelessly, gazing at no one.

"Sibyl," I urged, "I don't think it's good to see your body as the enemy. Can you try to forgive it? Can you put yourself on the same side as your body? You and your body against the cancer?"

"I don't know," she sighed. "I think maybe I don't really want to live."

"Oh, please live, Sibyl," I said, my eyes tearing. "We need you. Grace needs you." When Grace lived in New York, the two women saw each other every day.

She smiled wanly into the distance, seeing her dead husband, her dead son—or so I imagined. In November she died.

1992

OCTOBER—NOVEMBER—

DECEMBER

In October, my creatinine count was so low that they could not give me the cisplatin. This was a relief, but it also unnerved me. It meant that the first two doses had damaged my kidneys, perhaps irreparably. Nobody told me. That month, I met the radiologist Bruce Minsky, to whom I expressed my worries. He told me that only rarely can the whole protocol be given to any patient, and that the fluorouracil is if anything more potent than the more toxic drug. He insisted that radiation plus chemo should knock out any cancer that was left—he knew the tumor had disappeared. He also said I was a rarity, for in his many years of practice he had given radiation to only one or two people whose cancers had metastasized.

I did not know why my oncologist chose to break the pattern with me—he never spoke of it, and I forgot to ask him until 1997, when I ran across Bruce's statement in my notes. It was as I had guessed. An article in a medical journal I had read stated that a few patients with esophageal cancer survived more than a year when they received what the article called extremely severe treatment. "Severe" meant simultaneous chemotherapy and radiation. Although the article described only people whose cancers had not metastasized, it was decided to treat me this way.

The decision was based on the facts of my cancer. Cancers are rated by T (tumor), N (node), and M (metastasis). Tumors are rated by size between 1 and 4: mine was called a 2–3. Lymph nodes affected are rated N–0 or N–1: my affected lymph nodes were at some distance from the tumor but within the range the radiation would reach, so they were considered 0. Metastases may be 0 or 1, again depending on distance from the primary site. The metastasis of my tumor (apart from the lymph nodes) was very close to the original site and would automatically be affected by radiation. I therefore had a chance of living a little longer without my body being subjected to excessive radiation.

My October hospital stay was normal, except I was endowed with more guests than usual, all bubbling with optimism at my good news. The first day, Charlotte came, and that night, the coven appeared, complete with magic wands, eagle feathers, and candles I worried might set off the S-K smoke detectors. As she did each time she came, Gloria massaged my feet, something she excelled at. It was wonderfully relaxing. My old college friend Perry came the same night; the next day, I was visited by my three kids, my sister and her companion, Fred Baron, and my father (who lives near my sister), whom I had not seen since the Christmas before. Though eighty-six, he looked much younger; he was (and is) busy (he works several days a week) and relatively content despite his loneliness for my mother, then six years gone. He embraced me but could not speak. He kept shaking his head from side to side. At some point he muttered that he, not I, should be the one dying. I remember hearing my children's eighty-odd-year-old great-grandmother say the same thing when her son, their grandfather, died at fifty-nine. "It should have been me," she moaned. But whatever they say—and mean, at least consciously— those with the life force to survive to great ages cling to life with every pulse and breath of their bodies. Ida Demarest French lived well into her nineties; my father is now ninety-two.

Rob came again the next afternoon, and so did Carol; Gloria Beckerman visited on Friday, followed by Rosita Sarnoff and Beth Sapery—long-standing acquaintances who became friends during this period— and Linsey Abrams. On Saturday, Esther returned, and Jamie. It was—dare I say it?—almost too much. I need a goodly amount of solitude just to feel like myself. Still, my notes show that I revised twelve chapters of *Our Father* that week. They must not have needed much revision.

On Sunday, I was released—on time this month— and went back to the Mayflower. That night, I went out to dinner with the kids and Barbara's mother, Ruth, and her sister, Donna McKechnie, the great dancer. I remember we went to the Mackinac, a home-style restaurant on the West Side, chosen for its name—the McKechnies had lived in upper Michigan for years. I ordered macaroni and cheese, hoping I could eat something that soft; but I could not. I could only drink, and only water, apple juice, and tea. (I had been a coffee addict before; every morning I drank two cups of it made with the very best fresh-ground beans I could find, usually Celebes kalossi. Now coffee upset my insides; also anything with bubbles tortured my esophagus, and anything alcoholic burned it, as did acidic juices. At home, I often drank iced aloe vera and chamomile tea. I thought that if I survived, all this would vanish, but in fact it never did.) The mouth sores had already begun, on the *fifth* day after chemo this time. But this time, they lasted only a little over a week.

On Monday, I went to S-K for the first in a series of sessions to be measured for radiation. This lengthy process is undertaken to assure that the radiation will hit the affected area and only that area. Measured according to a formula the doctor has drawn up, you are marked with tiny tattoos that will guide the technicians when they move the machines around you.

My friends and children continued their faithful appearances; someone stayed with me every night—Rob and Barbara, Jamie, Carol, and Esther; Barbara Greenberg spent a day and night. I must have been feeling good, because my calendar is filled with movies, plays, lunches, and dinners I attended with a friend or my children. I saw Jim Silberman, my publisher; Florence Howe, a friend and the director of the Feminist

Press; a new friend, the playwright Janet Neipris; and my old friend Herb Weiss, as well as the coven and my kids. Someone drove me up to visit my friend LeAnne Schreiber in Ancram; we went to the jewel-box Ancram Opera House, which Melina Herring had turned into a successful theatrical enterprise. Despite all this, my memory of that time is permeated with dread and malaise; I was without joy in life. But perhaps I am projecting backward.

On October 26, I underwent the last preparation for radiation at S-K, and the next day I had my first session. The entire business is permeated with a sense of high seriousness: the technicians who work on you are pleasant enough but profoundly aware of the perils of radiation. A patient cannot but be extremely aware of the care they take, the anxiety that accompanies their placement of the machine, and the ceremony surrounding their swift evacuation of the room before the machine is turned on. You cannot avoid the realization that you are undergoing a procedure that is perhaps even more life-threatening than chemotherapy.

I was to have thirty sessions of radiation, altogether 5,000 rads. For the first segment of each session, I was instructed to lie on my back, while the technicians focused the machine directly on my esophagus, then angled in on it from the right, then the left side. The machine was angled this way so that the ray, shaped by the radiologist to spoon up, would not hit my spine. The spine cannot take more than 3,000 rads without severe damage. Then I was asked to turn over, and again the technicians moved the machine from one side to another. The whole process took about half an hour, and during it I felt nothing at all except anxiety—my own and that of the technicians. Indeed, when I first began to feel sick, I wondered if it was the atmosphere of that room that was affecting me. I thought it was all in my mind, because the radiation caused no sensation whatever. I felt nothing, or nothing I can describe: I felt bad but could not tell why. My experience was like that throughout the treatments—a creeping malaise that cannot be described because nothing in particular hurt, nor was there local debilitation beyond the burns. The next day, they started the chemo again.

I had told my oncologist that this arrangement worried me, that having radiation and chemotherapy at the same time would subject my body to too severe a punishment. In fact, the double whammy was the essential element of the treatment, but he never told me that. He pooh-poohed my anxiety, saying I was "a tough lady," unaware that he was belittling me, both by dismissing my objection as if it were not serious and by calling me a "lady." I did hypothesize (correctly) that the hardship of enduring chemo and radiation at the same time was intrinsic to the treatment, the element that made it "severe," the term used in the literature. But no one took the time to explain that to me. I would have accepted it despite my qualms; indeed, it is what I told myself. But by now I had come to trust my body; it had given me true information when medical science could not. And it was telling me that the double whammy was going to be too much for me. My body was right.

Again, I had many visitors. Gloria, learning that I

was not feeling well, sent a masseuse to the hospital to tone me up. The massage was wonderful, and I asked her to come again. Rob and Barbara came almost every day. We'd discuss how I felt and what they'd done that day or would be doing; then we sat gazing at one another. They looked worn and tired; I knew they were neglecting their lives for me—Barbara's school-work, Rob's exercise, their laundry and marketing, any leisure-time pleasures. I told them they did not have to come so often, but I'd been telling them that for months, uselessly. One day, I roused myself from my stuporous silence to say that it had been lovely to see them, that my eyes always drank them in thirstily, and that their visit had given me great pleasure, but now they should go home and get some rest.

"Huh?" Barbara asked, a little shocked. She does not always hear perfectly, and I tiredly began to repeat myself. But I did not make it all the way through before she began to laugh. "You know what I heard? I heard you say, 'Go home, you look a mess!'"

"Okay! Go home, you look a mess," I agreed, all of us laughing.

Afterward, that is what I would tell them whenever I felt they had put in enough time to calm their consciences. It became a family saying, a private joke.

On Sunday, I was released; Jamie came for me and we ate lunch, then I went home to rest. I returned to S-K every weekday after that for further radiation treatments, and every night someone came to stay with me—most often my children, Charlotte, or Esther. The mouth sores were not as severe as usual, and I was able to eat a bit, so had some energy. Linsey visited, and the two of us walked in Central Park for two and a half hours—of course, I had to take breaks. We had a wonderful conversation that gorgeous fall day: the temperature was mild, the trees still heavy and gorgeous with leaves, and all around us people walked and cycled in good humor. A few days later, I was happy to see my friend Lois Gould, back from Ireland on a visit.

But as time went on, visits became difficult because of my extreme enervation. When I was not on the radiation table, or getting to or from the hospital, I lay on the couch in my study. I neither wrote nor read. I think that much of the time I lay there in a partial daze, neither sleeping nor fully awake, on the edge of consciousness.

There are dates noted in my calendar—a gallery opening, a PEN meeting, a party, a talk by Christa Wolf, which I wanted very much to attend—but I attended none of them. I was too weak to do more than get myself to S-K every day, and even that was an effort. At some point, I asked Isabelle to accompany me, feeling unable even to manage the half-block walk from the hospital doors to First Avenue for a cab.

My sixty-third birthday arrived. Birthdays constitute a major holiday in our family, because we were all born around the same time: I on November 21, Jamie on November 22, and Rob on November 25. After my children were born, individual birthday parties became a thing of the past—although I've had some since, including the surprise party the kids gave for my fiftieth, featuring oysters and champagne. But even when the kids were little, they were feted together, like twins.

Sometimes I gave extra parties in the summer, inventing a June birth date, to spread out the celebration (and gifts) a bit. But within the family, the traditional event is a Thanksgiving dinner followed by an orgy of gift opening (sometimes we celebrate Barbara's birthday then too, instead of in August).

Happily, I had foreseen that I might feel ill by the time the birthdays came around, and had bought gifts in September and October. This year, Charlotte gave me a birthday dinner party. She wanted to please me, and perhaps she thought it would be my last, despite the good news of my CT scan. My condition at this time was not hopeful. She held the catered affair at my house, inviting my children, the coven, and her friend Miranda. The dinner looked delicious, but it was impossible for me to swallow; I had not been able to eat since the second week of radiation treatments. Since the radiation had also eradicated my appetite, I didn't miss food. What was harder was that I could barely sit up straight at the dinner table or converse with pleasure.

Back at the hospital on Monday, I told Dr. Minsky that I felt I was dying and asked him to stop the treatments. I said they could resume later, when I'd regained some strength. He was a sweet man and didn't pooh-pooh my fears, but he denied that I was in fact dying. He did not, however, ask why I thought I was dying. I took it mine was a common reaction. The radiation continued. I spent my days at S-K or on my couch. I no longer encouraged people to visit.

The kids arranged a Thanksgiving feast, inviting my father and Barbara's sister Donna. I have little memory of it; I could not eat and was miserable sitting up and having to talk. But I tried.

Two days later, I had to return to S-K for my final course of chemo. I went in like someone on dead man's walk—stolid, silent, uncomplaining, but sunk within myself as I approached the execution chamber. My demeanor could not have been more different from the determined cheer with which I entered the hospital the first time. This was probably predictable. But I didn't think about the future then and was thinking about it even less now. Like most people, I thought about coping; many of us spend our whole lives this way, never considering more than getting through the next ordeal. We protect ourselves from our wretched experiences by not feeling them, by letting ourselves feel only a stoic determination to survive. Maybe this behavior works to our advantage in crises, but in many situations it stands between us and living our lives.

Enervation had turned me into a docile patient, helpless, caught, trapped in a system. I felt that the doctors were caught in it, too. The department, the hospital, the huge system, encompassed us all, and nothing could be done about it. They were killing me, and I was letting them. There was no way to stop it.

I was to have the usual six days of chemotherapy, and five more radiation treatments. But in the end I didn't.

I was sitting in a wheelchair, waiting in a corridor of the radiology department for my appointment, when Bruce Minsky came up and said I was not to go in. He was stopping my treatments after all. I thought he had decided to take my advice.

"Why?" I asked.

"You have serious third-degree burns on your chest. I can't risk exacerbating them."

I had been using the recommended lotion on my chest, but lotions are useless against radiation burns. The only good thing about them was they didn't hurt much. It was a painless form of death.

Bruce argued with me as if I had complained; he was really having a dialogue with himself, clearly worried that calling an early halt to treatment might vitiate my chances to recover. He said that I would miss only five treatments; I had fulfilled most of the recommended course. He insisted the radiation would have done its work. But as far as I was concerned, he could have been speaking into the wind. I was past caring.

As I look back now, the process surrounding radiation seems absurd, sort of like building air raid shelters against nuclear bombs or wearing a cheesecloth face mask when dealing with toxic waste. The doctor and the technicians worked so hard beforehand, making so many calculations; they calibrated treatments as if they really knew what dosage damages organs, bones, and skin; they tried to ensure that the X ray would be directed at the correct spot. All this took hours, as I lay on the hard table under the machine, cold, hurting, and patient. And for what? The calibrations are a joke: radiation is lethal. It was hitting my esophagus, yes, but also my spine, my heart, my brain stem, and my lower jaw. And the effects of radiation continue until you die: they never stop. I am affected still, and I never know what will be hit next. In later years, as, one by one, parts of my body collapsed and I saw various S-K specialists, each of them would say: Well, you didn't really have enough radiation / chemotherapy to cause this damage, but it seems to have (1) destroyed the cerebellar balance center in the brain, (2) damaged your heart, (3) destroyed your spinal column, (4) damaged your salivary glands, (5) destroyed the peripheral nerves in your feet or fingers, etc., etc.

I received Bruce's news passively, but I was deeply relieved that the ordeal was over. I had a weak hope that in fact I would not die but might, once the radiation was over with, be able to regain some strength. I completed the chemo course, my last, and on Friday, December 4, was released. But that night, I ran a fever high enough for Urgent Care to require me to come in. I was hospitalized for a couple of days, then the fever fell and they released me again.

One day, feeling improved, I gave my situation some thought. So far, the tumor had not returned. I had finished chemotherapy and radiation, and although I felt terrible, chances were I would feel better eventually. Surely I would be better in a month, I thought. I decided to concentrate on getting better. I made a *decision* to get better. For the first time in months, I sat down at my desk and picked up the telephone. I called my travel agent and asked her to make reservations at a luxury hotel in Key West for early January: I would take the children down there for a lovely rest and some sun. They deserved a treat after their ordeal. Then I called to arrange for my car to be transported to Florida for the season.

I noted these arrangements in my calendar. They are the only marks for the month. Apart from that one day, I was too ill to keep records, too ill even to think of writing anything down. There were days when I did not even get out of bed, something I had avoided all during chemotherapy, although I was told that some people take to their beds during treatment. I had always gotten up, dressed, even put on eye makeup. I had sat at dinner tables, whether or not I could eat.

No more. I still dressed, but I did little else. I rarely bothered to put on my wig; I'd grown used to my bald head. Unable to eat, I had no reason to sit at a table. I didn't read or watch television. I did listen to music and the radio, especially *Performance Today* on WNYC. I slept and simply lay there, in bed or on my couch, empty of head and heart. I was supposed to speak at a conference at Hofstra University in November or December, and at the 92nd Street Y in December, but I had to cancel both. The only times I left the house were when Urgent Care demanded I come in because of my fever.

Between December 4 (the day I was released after my last chemo course) and December 10 or 11, I was in and out of Urgent Care and Memorial Sloan-Kettering Hospital several times, with fever and low white cell counts. On about the twelfth of the month, the doctors said I had to stay in the hospital until they got the fever down. Sepsis, manifested by fever, frequently kills chemotherapy patients, who lack enough white cells to fight infection.

I saw a host of doctors in this period; most were infectious disease specialists trying to find medications for stubborn problems like mine. (This specialty seems to attract especially pleasant people.) They tried one antibiotic after another, but none seemed to work for more than a day or two. The fever went up and down, but it never went away.

In all this time, my primary oncologist did not visit me. I had not seen him since my outpatient appointment on November 10. I do not know if he was even aware I was sick. He rarely made hospital rounds, because he was often away during his supposed month on duty. He traveled a great deal, giving speeches at medical conferences, no doubt pertaining to his work on a cancer cure. I would have liked to see him, because I felt I needed to consult someone who had a larger view of my illness than simply my fever, someone who could evaluate my overall condition. I did not know who else to turn to.

My biggest problem in this period was starvation. I could not eat and could drink only water, weak tea, apple juice, and aloe vera. But I was being hydrated through my IV line. When I was home, I could occasionally get some soup down (my kids and my friends made soups for me, out of thoughtfulness and love), and I drank the vegetable juices the kids prepared. And while the kids brought me food I could keep in the hospital refrigerator and heat in the microwave of the floor kitchen, I lacked the energy to do so. Even if I got something down, it wasn't enough. I had lost about thirty pounds and smilingly told the doctors I was starving; they smiled back. Jamie bought me a pin to attach to my velour tops; it said, in great big letters, I WANT FOOD! But no one suggested that I be fed through my IV line; nor did I suggest it. I was waiting for the doctors to do so. My weakness seems to have affected my brain. Maybe the doctors weren't aware that my esophagus was ulcerated from radiation. No one was watching over my whole person. Not even me.

When the fever dipped, I would feel instantly better and immediately imagine that I would continue to feel better, that I was on my way to recovery. In such a state, I determined to attend the coven's equinox celebration and had Isabelle bring me a black velvet pantsuit, black heels, and jewelry. I cajoled the doctors into giving me permission to leave the hospital that evening, and the nice guy who finally gave it said, "Okay, if you want to. But I wouldn't think you'd be able to." He was right. As the time to dress approached, I realized that I could not even face getting up and putting on my fancy clothes, much less going outside in the cold weather, walking to First Avenue, and hailing a cab.

But when I thought about Christmas, I determined that nothing would stop me. Since they were born, nearly forty years before, I had never not been with my children on Christmas Eve. I was not going to spend Christmas in a hospital bed, I insisted. Again I spoke to the doctors, who were leery—"You're not ready to go home"—but bending. "Well," one said, "you'd have to have home nurses to keep the IV going, and home nurses are not always great. But the chances are you wouldn't get great care in the hospital, either, over Christmas." If they could find home nurses for me, they said finally, I could go home. They did. I called the kids in triumph.

The antibiotic they were giving me wasn't working, and they decided to switch to Ceftazidime, one of the cephalosporins connected to the penicillin family.

They may have given me a dose or two before I left the hospital—I'm not sure—but the day I was to leave, I felt terrific, relatively speaking. I had some energy and was in high spirits. Packed and ready to leave, I was waiting for Isabelle to arrive when my friend Ann Jones came to visit me. She was back from one of her adventurous jaunts across the world, and we were both feeling high. She offered to teach me an exercise that would help me regain my muscle strength without putting too much of a strain on my weakened body, so we went upstairs to the penthouse lounge, which was always empty and had a broad carpeted floor. Briefly disconnected from the IV, I felt as coltish as an emancipated slave. I did the exercise with no trouble and had energy left over. Then I went home to celebrate Christmas.

My spirits fell almost instantly on getting home. The kids had not had time to decorate, and not expecting me, Isabelle had not bought flowers. The apartment looked dreary (although it was cleaned twice a week) and unlived-in. I felt suddenly very bad. My energy had drained as swiftly and unexpectedly as a tornado arrives, and I sat on the couch in my study, feeling glum. One of the nurses arrived—a man. The one male nurse who had tended me at S-K was the only nasty, peremptory nurse I ever encountered there, so I viewed this man with wariness. Though he was pleasant, he had a funny odor, which I quickly realized was urine. I could not bear to have him near me and kept protesting to the children, "He smells of urine!" They said he didn't; they said I was imagining it. But years later, when we were talking about him, Jamie agreed: he smelled of urine. By then, I wasn't sure whether this was because he did smell of urine and they had been denying it, or she was remembering my perception rather than her own. In any case, *I* smelled it, and it was disgusting. He hung the bags on a pole and connected the IV to my arm, just as in the hospital but without the blue box that controlled the flow. As I sat there with the antibiotic dripping into my vein, I felt truly ill. My eyes would not focus, and light hurt them. Any light source blurred into a halo, and whenever I tried to focus on anything, my head would ache.

I may have eaten something—who knows? Soup, perhaps. But I felt worse and worse. When the nurse prepared me for bed, replacing an empty antibiotic bag with a new one, I said, "I think I'm allergic to this antibiotic. It makes me feel awful." He said nothing, and I presumed he dismissed my remark.

Nowadays, of course, I would jump up and down and scream, "Stop this IV! Call the doctor and tell him I'm allergic to it!" But that is hindsight.

When I was a child, my family celebrated Christmas Eve, not Christmas Day, which was an anticlimax. Our family used to join my mother's sister's family for the major celebration of the year, and one of my uncles would arrive on the stroke of midnight wearing a Santa Claus outfit and carrying a pillowcase filled with gifts. We continued this practice in our adulthood, my sister and I with our children, my father playing Santa Claus. Nowadays we dressed up on Christmas Eve, had a celebratory feast, often with friends, and afterward exchanged gifts. That year of 1992, I have some memory of our small family sitting in the living room, probably dressed up; I don't recall food. I don't know whether I had gifts for the children. But I do remember Jamie's gift to me.

When I planned the gardens for my Berkshire house, I put a weeping beech tree on the lawn in front of the woods that line the property. I envisioned that in years to come (after I was dead), the tree would spread across the grassy plain like a huge glowing umbrella. The tree grew very slowly, however, and five years later, it suddenly died. My gardener had the soil tested, and we hypothesized about problems with the site, but after she took the root to the local gardening center (in the Berkshire Mountains, there are still people who know about plants), she said it was the chance of the graft—weeping beeches are not a natural form but a hybrid. She urged me to try again.

I refused. I had been too disappointed by the first failure of a tree I had such dreams for: I felt the tree and the site were unlucky. But she continued to urge it, and a year later, I finally gave in. The second weeping beech lasted no more than two years. Now, despite the gardener's urgings, I was adamant. The spot remained an empty hole in the middle of the lawn.

Jamie had ordered, not a weeping beech, but a chestnut tree. She remembered how much I had loved the row of chestnuts that lined the avenue leading to a house we'd lived in years before—especially when they bloomed in the spring. She suggested that we put the new tree in a spot to the right and rear of where the weeping beech had been. It would be planted in spring.

"You think I'm going to live to see it flower?" I asked, smiling and wiping away tears.

"You will," she promised.

It flowered this year.

The next day was Christmas, and people came: my father, my sister and Fred, as well as the kids. Other people stopped in, I can't remember who, though I know Rosita and Beth were there for a while. The kids had made a dinner and served it buffet style, I think. I could not eat, although I remember them bringing me a plate. I could barely sit in the chair. Everyone hurt my eyes, and talking was truly painful. I was so uncomfortable, I wanted to cry. But I must not have seemed too sick, because Beth told me recently that they thought I was angry with my family, my father and sister, that I sounded angry when I spoke. I remembered, then, hearing the irritation in my voice. Indeed, I was irritated, but with my condition, not with any person. Interesting that I took it out on my father and sister, the ones who had known me when I was little.

I can't say whether it was that night or the next that things got so bad. Nor can I tell you what was wrong, precisely, except that my body was miserably uncomfortable with itself and could not be eased. I may have called the doctor; or perhaps one of the children did. Perhaps it was at this time that they prescribed morphine, which I took through the IV and which made me sick. I cannot remember anything except the misery of being inside my body. This sensation grew particularly strong as I was going to bed. I asked the nurse to move my limbs to make me more comfortable, and he did, but he wasn't able to help me and grew annoyed with my demands. So after he'd given me a strong sleeping medication, I told him to ask my son to come upstairs. I asked Rob to move my legs one way and another, and he did, sweetly. Nothing seemed to help.

I looked up at him. "I've never felt so bad in my whole life," I said. He doesn't remember that, but it's the last thing I remember.

OUT OF TIME

Swimming up through the velvety dark, I heard them. Their voices sounded joyous, and I was overjoyed to hear them.

"Hi, kids," I said.

I couldn't see them, but I could hear the three of them clamoring, "Hi, Mom," "Hi, Mara," talking excitedly. I know I was smiling.

"Are you having a party?"

"Party?"

"No, no party."

"Why do you think . . . ?"

"Why does she think . . . ?"

"You sound so happy. How come you're so happy? It sounds as if you're having a party." There was so much noise, so many people, the kids were so bubbly. Who was there? Where were we? Were all those people in my house? Everyone sounded in high spirits. "Who are all the people?"

Rob answered. "Oh, they're just technicians and nurses, you know." I didn't know; it made no sense to me. I heard music.

"There's music," I argued.

"It's just the TV," he explained.

TV? In my house? When there were people visiting? That didn't sound right. I was too tired to press it, but I knew something must be going on that they were not telling me about. They were too happy for it to be just an ordinary day. Jamie sounded happy in a particular way.

"And Jamie's in love," I said. I could hear it in her voice.

"I don't *believe* it!" she cried loudly, and stomped off. I smiled.

I was being pulled up out of the darkness by noise, a metallic clamor. I pushed it away, but it was too intrusive and drove itself into my consciousness. I listened.

TV! I gasped silently. Men's voices oppressively shrieking, shouting, exhorting, harsh on my ears, cajoling, harassing, urging, arguing, pressuring, insisting, watch this program, buy this product, great buy, bargain, go to wonderland, do that!!!!! I couldn't stand it. I don't want to be in this world, I thought, pushing for the depths again, diving as hard as I could. The voices followed me for a while. It was a long time before I could blot them out, escape to the other world, where there was no TV. With relief, I regained the velvety underwater silence.

I could see, but only a little. My vision was blurry, but it looked like Gloria standing in front of me.

"Marilyn," she said softly, "there are an awful lot of people here. Would you prefer that we keep them outside and just let them in one by one?"

"Yes, thanks," I said. I didn't think *outside where* or wonder why so many people were there, wherever *there* was. Somehow, I knew I was in a hospital. But in truth I didn't want to see anyone. I couldn't see well. I would have to converse if there were people, and it hurt me to talk. There was something in my throat. And when I talked, saliva came pouring out of the corner of my mouth. I didn't want anyone to see that: I'd be embarrassed. And I was too tired to talk to people. But I didn't want to say that to Gloria; it sounded rude. I couldn't imagine her saying a thing like that; she wouldn't understand. I didn't want her to see the saliva, either. But she was gone.

No one came. I could go back to sleep. Thank heavens.

A number of people were standing in my room. I knew them all—there were the kids, there was the coven, and over there, my sister and my father. Others, too . . . who? A head poked around the corner and peered in. It was Beth Sapery. People turned and looked at her. I wasn't sure anyone knew her. I couldn't recall whether the kids had met her. I was afraid she did not know anyone and would feel strange. She stepped into the room, looking a bit uneasy. I raised my head a little. "Hi, Beth. Come in," I said, trying to inform the others that she was a friend, so they would welcome her. Then I lay back down and rested. I was so tired.

Note dated 1/11/93, in Rob's handwriting:
Girl Gang visited: recognized all and conversed.
Bella Abzug visited: recognized and conversed.
LeAnne visited: recognized and conversed.
Charlotte & Miranda
Ann Jones
Regula (an old acquaintance who worked with Charlotte)

Note dated 1/12/93, in Rob's handwriting:
Didn't remember anyone who visited yesterday.
Introducing Dr. Minsky (radiologist): "He's the one who tried to kill me. He's nice despite what he does."
Thought [Dr.] Renny Griffith was Daniel.

"Good morning!"
"Ummm."
"How are we this morning?"
"Ummm."
"So, do you know where you are?"
Silence.

"Do you know what year it is?"
"1945."

Note dated 1/13/93, in Jamie's handwriting:
"Do you know where you are?"
"Yonkers."
"No. You're in New York. Do you know what
building this is?"
"The Science Capital of the World."
"Do you know what year it is?"
"1963."

"Good morning!"
"Morning."
"Do you know where you are?"
"No."
"Do you know what year it is?"
"Certainly."
"Well, what year is it?"
"I'm not going to tell *you*!"
Subdued laughter, not mine.
"Do you know who the President is?"
"Of course. Clinton." Spoken with hauteur.
Barbara M. leaped into the air, her arm raised in a
cheering salute. "Yay!" she cried.
It was then that I understood something was wrong.

Recollections of Carol Jenkins:
"Carol! Today I saw my own mind for the first time!"

"Guess who I saw when I was dead! The editor of the *James Joyce Quarterly*. John!" I went on about this John.

Joint recollection of the coven:
CAROL: "We did a ceremony around your bed. We had the usual equipment—feathers, wands, beads. . . ."
ESTHER: "They didn't want us in there. They frowned at us, and I was afraid they'd throw us out."
GLORIA: "No, it was just that patients were not supposed to have more than one guest at a time."
ESTHER: "Two, I think."
GLORIA: "But we went in anyway. We just went in. But I was worried about the man in the next bed. I thought if he suddenly woke up and saw us hovering over you with all our stuff, he might have a heart attack."
Later, GLORIA: "We were always convinced you would recover. We knew it. Because you were always you. You were always present, you were there. Other people I've seen in comas were absent."

It was dark. I was in a hospital room. I was alone. I had to pee. The toilet was only a few feet from the bed; its door was open. I decided to get up. I tried to sit but found it difficult. It took a while. Then I saw that the bed had a railing, a foot or so higher than the mattress. I tried, but somehow I could not lift my legs over it. I kept trying until, exhausted, I fell back. Glancing down, I could see that the railing did not extend the full length of the mattress. If I could crawl to the foot of the bed, maybe I could climb out there. I began to move.

For some reason, it was hard for me to move on this mattress. I toiled and toiled but barely inched forward. To move at all, I had to propel myself with great heaves. It was a very long time before I arrived at the foot of the bed. I put my legs out to step over—and suddenly fell flat on the floor. I was lying on my stomach, my face mashed into the cold floor. Leaning on my hands, I tried to raise my body. It didn't move. I tried to raise my head to see if there was anyone in the corridor outside who could help me, but when I raised it, my head fell—hard—back onto the hospital floor, squashing my nose. Near tears, I tried again to raise my head. Again, it smashed onto the floor. My nose hurt. I began to cry softly. I did not understand why I could not raise my head. I called out for help, but my voice was weak and faint, as in a nightmare. After a time, someone heard me.

"Oh, my God!" the woman called out to another, who ran into the room.

"Where's her nurse!"

I was lifted up.

"I have to pee," I said faintly, and was helped to the toilet.

"Where is your nurse?" the woman cried.

I didn't know. I didn't know I had a nurse.

There was much ado, and after a time, a young woman ran into the room. "Oh, I only left her for a minute!" she cried, near tears. "I just went down for some coffee!"

I said nothing, although I knew she'd been gone for a long time. I didn't care. I didn't care what she did. What I cared about was my helplessness. What was the matter with me? Why couldn't I do anything? I couldn't even move by myself! *What was wrong?*

1992–1993

DECEMBER—JANUARY—

FEBRUARY

It was Sunday night, December 27, 1992, when I said to Rob, "I've never felt so bad in my whole life." Yearning for relief from discomfort, I sought sleep; thanks to a sedative, it soon came. But that sleep did not end for a long time. My next memory is of a moment over two weeks later, when I woke hearing my kids' happy voices. The interim was anguish for them.

The Monday after Christmas, Jamie and Barbara went to work as usual. Rob stayed with me: worried, my son decided not to go to work that day. The nurse was unable to wake me in the morning but said nothing until about eleven, when she told Rob of the problem. He came into my room, sat on the edge of the bed, and called, "Mom," several times. He touched me; I did not respond. He called more loudly; he shook my shoulder. He put his arm around me and tried to pull me up, but I simply sank back. Suddenly, I sat straight up, eyes open, arms stretched out, but said nothing. He rubbed my back, asked if I was okay; when his hand moved to my lower back, near the kidney, I flinched and mumbled in pain. Sitting beside me, he turned my body so my legs hung to the floor. He put his arm around me, and my head fell to his shoulder.

The nurse came into the room and asked Rob if he wanted her to call an ambulance. He said yes. As he sat there with me, waiting for its arrival, the telephone rang. It was Carol, wanting to know how I was. "Not too good," Rob said. Unsure whether I could hear him, and fearful of upsetting me or Carol, he watched his words.

"We can't seem to rouse her," he said.

"What do you mean, you can't rouse her!" she cried.

"Well, she won't wake up."

"Call an ambulance! Get her to the hospital right away!" Carol directed, saying she'd meet him there.

Then Rob called Jamie. Again, he spoke warily, so warily that Jamie did not at first understand the situation was serious. Once she did, she agreed to meet him at Urgent Care.

The nurse announced the arrival of the ambulance. They put me in slippers and a robe; attendants carried a reclining stretcher chair up to the bedroom. They had to get me down a winding staircase to the front door and the elevator. Rob traveled with me in the ambulance. Carol was already at S-K when we arrived. The Urgent Care nurses called my name to see if I would respond. Nothing. But when they pinched me, I yelled "Ouch!" After than, however, I sank deeper into unconsciousness. They kept me in the corridor until a bed opened up—quite a while, Rob recalls. They summoned what Rob called a "baby neurologist," an inexperienced doctor, who used a metal instrument to determine my level of response. Rob was disgusted: "It was obvious that you weren't responding at all. He was like someone playing with a toy, trying to seem important, when all he had to do was look." The doctor may have felt Rob's scorn, for he asked him to leave.

Rob called Barbara, went to the bank for money to pay the ambulance attendants, then sat in the corridor, waiting, with Jamie, Carol, and, later, Barbara. He called Charlotte, Esther, and Gloria, but they were all away over the holidays. He called my sister.

Jamie came in to see me, and while she stood there, I had a seizure: my whole body shook in a convulsion, horrifying her. Hours passed. A nurse came out and told them I was being moved to the SCU (Special Care Unit), S-K's intensive care. The kids followed me there. Rob thinks a woman doctor came out and spoke to them, but because no one could tell them anything definite, they have only vague memories of the doctors. Eventually, a nurse told them to go home, saying I was "stable" and that someone would call if any important change occurred.

But they would not move. They stayed with me the rest of that day and the next. For two nights running, they slept on the floor of the SCU waiting room, using their coats as mattresses. They recall the waiting room as pleasant; it was carpeted and had comfortable couches. When I visited it recently—having no memory of it—it was tiled, no longer carpeted, but on the floor were the mattress and rumpled sheets of another faithful watcher. The present chairs do not look comfortable. I am glad it was carpeted when they slept there. The nurses, more wonderful here even than elsewhere in that hospital, brought them pillows, sheets, and blankets. Carol stayed until about 4:00 a.m. Tuesday, went home to check on her family, and returned at 8:00 a.m. with doughnuts and coffee.

The kids were constant presences, although after the second night, they slept at my apartment, all three of them. If an emergency arose, Rob and Barbara would have been too far away if they had gone home to Staten Island. Jamie lived closer, in the Village, yet she stayed with her brother and her old friend Barbara. I like to think of the three of them together, ready to comfort each other if I died. They brought in the charms I had hung around my bed at home and hung them over my hospital bed. They brought the little radio with earphones that I had used for visualization tapes, and played tapes of music they knew I liked. Days they spent beside me, speaking to me, stroking my hand. They acted as hosts for my guests in the SCU waiting room and became part of a small community of waiters and watchers. Toward the end of my stay in the Special Care Unit, they found some kind of hand-held computer game, calculator size, which they fought over and took turns with. It became a constant presence with them—especially Jamie—and they played with it obsessively. It had the advantage of blanking out everything in the world but itself.

From what various sources have told me, every part of my body was hooked up to some machine. I was on life support: a respirator with a tube down my throat, a catheter in my urethra, IV lines in my arms, a heart monitor attached to my chest. Jamie recalls the Venodyne boots that kept circulation going in my feet and lower legs by imposing pressure every few minutes. I had brain seizures, for which they gave me Dilantin. When I went back to examine the room I occupied then, I saw why I once called it the "Science Capital of the World." Each SCU cubicle is filled with machines, tens of them, of all sorts, mounted one above the other in a series of tall columns. The only thing missing on my recent visit was the TV set, an intrusive presence when I was comatose. As I went deeper into coma, my kidneys failed and I blew up into a "beached whale," Charlotte says. My tongue became bloody and swelled so it no longer fit in my mouth. I was a pasty white color.

The kind nurses, doubtless moved by my children's devotion, called every morning to tell them how I was, so they need not rush in. One nurse in particular, Colette, won my children's love and respect by her tender, solicitous care of me. She gave them more information than any of the doctors, saying, "People don't generally come out of comas like this," but also that people as badly off as I was had been known to walk out of the SCU. Everyone describes the care I received as superb. "People were working on you all the time," Gloria recalls. "They measured your fluid intake and output, they checked to see if your bone marrow was suppressed, they had to clear your tubes regularly, they monitored all the instruments, you had a heart monitor, a respirator. . . ."

But no one told the children what was wrong with me. This was not obfuscation: no one knew. The kids made sure to be present during the doctors' rounds, but the only information they were given concerned counts and medications. Rob remembers an SCU doctor, Renny Griffith, as especially kind and efficient. I went back in 1997 and tried to thank him and Colette; neither of them worked there any longer.

But the doctor in charge of the SCU was a different story. He had never seen me before, and the kids did not know him, but one day he came striding in. A "distant superior aloof supercilious arrogant bastard hotshot full of his own brilliance stood in the middle of the room to make his authoritative medical judgment," my son says in fury, even now, five years later. He loudly announced that I had stopped breathing during the night, that the cancer had spread to the brain stem, and that I was dead. There was nothing they could do.

Jamie went to pieces: she wailed, screamed, stamped her feet. Rob comforted her. But with part of their minds, they refused to believe him. A few days later, Esther was visiting when the kids saw this doctor walking down the hall. They pointed him out, explaining what he had done. Esther stopped short to listen, then chased after him. Returning after a while, she smiled broadly and said she'd taken care of him.

"What did you do?"

"I put a spell on him," she said.

"Oh, good!" Jamie cheered. "The big tall guy?"

"Uh-oh," says Esther. She had taken on a short guy with a beard and glasses. Since Esther's infliction of the evil eye had had satisfyingly catastrophic results on previous occasions, she has been worried since.

Rob, Jamie, and Barbara must have been glazed with boredom and worry. They lived in the SCU waiting room: they were there for most of the day, every day. They played a hand-held computer game to which all three became addicted; they chatted with my visitors, all of whom they knew; and with their own friends, who came to see me out of love for them. And they made friends with the family of a fifteen-year-old boy, Brandon, suffering from neuroblastoma, a rare cancer of nerve endings. The family lived in a small town in Illinois that had been plagued with this rare disease: four children had been diagnosed with it. Staying in New York was a drain on the family; the parents and grandparents took turns sleeping in a single hotel room to save money. Both wanted to stay with their beloved child, whose immediate problem was sepsis. Emotions flourish in such situations, and my children and Esther, on one hand, and the boy's family, especially his grandparents, on the other, grew to love one another.

Rob went through aphaeresis, a two-and-a-half hour transfusion of white blood cells, to help the boy. In this unpleasant process, all the blood is gradually drained from the body through one arm, passed through a separator that filters out the white cells, and then returned to the other arm. The family asked

Esther to perform a ritual over the child, which she did burdened with anxiety and a sense of ineffectuality. She had no confidence in her powers with him—and indeed, the child died.

On March 28, 1998, the *New York Times* ran a short piece reporting that the company that cleaned up coal tar at an abandoned plant owned by the Central Illinois Public Service Company of Springfield had been ordered to pay $3 million to the four families whose children were stricken—including Brandon's. The company, now called Amerencips, of course plans to appeal. In any case, it is too late for Brandon and his family.

Charlotte and Barbara G. were appalled at the machines, the tubes, and my general condition, knowing how I would hate my situation if I could see myself. Both had heard my impassioned diatribes against medical technology; both knew I did not want to live hooked up to machines. But apparently, neither of them spoke to the children about this (the kids do not have any memory of such a conversation; my friends' memories are equally vague). My two tough-minded friends did talk to each other, deploring a situation in which neither felt she could legitimately intervene.

Despite the universal medical opinion that I was as good as dead, no doctor or nurse suggested taking me off the machines. Rob had a copy of my living will, but he says he didn't think about it at all, and when one of my friends—not Charlotte or Barbara—did say something to him about pulling the plug, he was angry with her. He did not want to receive such suggestions. Neither of my children remembered the conversation at the outset of my illness in which I told them that I had made a pact with Charlotte to disconnect me if it became necessary. But I think that they—or at least Rob—had given it some unconscious thought and dismissed the idea, for when we discuss it now, he protests that no one knew what was wrong with me, no one knew whether I'd recover or not, and the fact that they did not expect me to recover did not mean I wouldn't. I wasn't brain dead; that my brain was riddled with cancer was, as far as Rob was concerned, only one (disgusting) man's opinion. There was no reason to pull the plug, my son insists.

But I wonder what I would have done if I had been the one standing beside an inert friend whose doctors all agreed she was as good as dead and who had begged me beforehand to act in such an eventuality. I do not know what I would have done before this experience. *Now* is a different story. For I will never again be certain about what constitutes hopelessness or precisely when machines become instruments of hell.

Barbara Greenberg has a friend, Tracy, whose three-and-a-half-year-old boy fell from a window in an upper story of her house when he was in the care of a nanny. He went into a coma, and all the doctors gave up on him (this was thirty-odd years ago), insisting the situation was hopeless. But not Tracy. Being fortunate enough to have help to care for her three other children, she spent every day at the hospital. She brought tapes of the other children talking to him, books and music she read aloud and played, while touching and caressing the boy. He remained comatose for several weeks, but eventually, contrary to the doctors' expectations, he woke up. He required months of rehabilitation, but in time he largely recovered. He had to wear a helmet when he rode his bike—something all children do now—and he retained some damage on one side of his body. But he is alive and otherwise quite well now, a man in his thirties.

Most of us know at least one such story. We also know others—especially with the advances in technology—of people who were kept alive by machines way past the point of humanity. But we have means now to detect when someone is brain dead—which they did not have in the days when Tracy tended her child. And it seems to me that this is what's crucial.

My dear Barbara M. recently suffered a similar situation with her mother, Ruth. During an operation for a problem of the digestive system, the surgeon found cancer and took tissue for biopsies. Ruth's doctors, being human, were uncertain: five of them seemed to feel there was little hope; the oncologist urged chemotherapy; the nurses, whom the McKechnie children placed trust in (because they had developed a relationship with Ruth), also seemed to oppose it. But no one made open suggestions or spoke directly to the problem—Ruth's children had to depend on innuendo and facial expression. Chemotherapy was started. But Barbara, uncertain about what to do, sank into an anxious depression, having, on the one hand, an ardent desire that her mother recover and, on the other, a fervent desire to protect her from pain. And Ruth was in great pain. The doctors put her on high doses of painkillers, which rendered her unconscious.

When Barbara asked my opinion, I could not urge her to pull the plug, despite her mother's pain and the humiliation and indignity of her bodily state. I had become unsure. Barbara remained in a state of high anxiety for days, until she learned that Ruth had cancer throughout her body—her liver, bones, and pancreas—and that her surgeon placed her chances for recovering even from the original surgery at ten to fifteen percent. Only then, and with extreme grief, were her children able to make a decision to stop the chemotherapy. When the doctors told them that all of Ruth's systems were failing, they stopped the respirator and the intravenous feeding—everything but the morphine. The doctors said she would live only an hour or two, but Ruth clung to life. Two days after they removed the respirator, after a three-week ordeal, she died.

My children faced even greater confusion, for all the doctors were convinced I would die, yet none could say with certainty what was wrong with me or that whatever it was was lethal. And in fact, I was not riddled with cancer; I did not have cancer of the brain, as some doctors assumed. I was not doomed to death; it only seemed so.

Unsure about what was wrong with me, the doctors debated my treatment among themselves. The newest and youngest member of the gastrointestinal group, David Ilson, urged giving me dialysis. There were sufficient medical reasons against this, but in time perhaps they felt there was nothing to lose. I had no personal relation with any of the doctors who treated me (my primary oncologist was not one of them), nor did any of them later speak with me regarding the coma, but these physicians were as dedicated and care-ful as one could wish. I remember one older man, a nephrologist or urologist, who came to my room a few weeks after I woke up to tell me he was recommending that I not continue dialysis. Since I had decided that if I had to continue it, I would end my life, I was greatly relieved: he had, essentially, given me back my life (however temporarily). But what moved me about him, what I remember still, was his delight at the fact that I did not need this miserable treatment, that I would be freed of it. And in fact, the dialysis had turned the trick. Soon after my first treatment, I began to wake up. I had been in a coma for twelve days.

My oncologist visited me only once during this time, at the very end. He did not seek out my children when he left, but they spotted him and ran after him as he walked toward the elevators. When they caught up, he was pleasant enough but told them little. He explained that the doctors were not sure what had happened to me. Possibly, he suggested, I had had an allergic reaction to the antibiotic. Rob blamed the medical establishment for that, but the oncologist shrugged. One out of 250,000 people was allergic to cephalosporins, he said. How could they predict? By the time I was told this, the figure was one out of 400,000. I do not know which, if either, is correct.

But in conversations since, he has explained to me that reactions like mine simply do not occur in cases of allergy. Allergies may cause a rash, swelling of the mouth or other organs, and some life-threatening symptoms, but not brain seizures, which I was having constantly. He now hypothesizes that whatever caused the brain seizures also killed any cancer left in me: in other words, he is suggesting that the coma on which for a long time I blamed my subsequent problems was actually responsible for my survival of cancer. Since he did not describe the nature of what could have caused the seizures, I cannot quite understand the logic of this, but I assume there is some. Moreover, he said, people don't survive comas like mine: I was on advanced life support, without which I would have died. People who suffer such brain seizures do not as a rule recover. Everything is a mystery.

On the twelfth day of my coma, early in the morning, a nurse called the children to say I had shown slight improvement; my eyelids had flickered. I might be starting to wake up. Excited, they tore over to the hospital, but I was dead as a stone. During the next day or two, they could see I was still having brain seizures. I think they lost heart. Then one day, I heard their voices. My eyes were closed; I could not open them: perhaps they were glued shut by oozing matter. I could not see the children, but I heard them, and I said, "Hi, kids." They crowed hellos. I wondered why they were so happy.

The fragmented memories I retain come from this period: waking up hearing the children, seeing Gloria standing by my bed and hearing her question, the sense that there was something in my throat (it was the respirator tube), seeing Beth Sapery enter the room, the doctors and their morning interrogations. Reading over the children's note saying I thought Renny Griffith was "Daniel," I was confounded: I don't know any Daniel. Nor do I know any John in charge of the *James Joyce*

Quarterly, nor any man by that name important in the Joyce Society. Jamie insisted I had seen John Lennon in the great beyond, but she was the one who had stood for hours in front of the Dakota, grieving for him, not I. I do remember "seeing my own mind," as I told Carol. It had to do with levels of consciousness.

My friends believed I was "conscious" when they came to see me after I awoke from the coma, yet I have no memory of these visits. My only memories are the fragments I included in the previous chapter, all that is left of about a week's events *after* I "regained consciousness." I hypothesized that there are two levels of consciousness—consciousness and self-consciousness—and that without the second, there is no memory. We are conscious in infancy and young childhood, yet we remember only a couple of vital moments, if anything, because we are not conscious of ourselves as separate people, as people watching ourselves act, hearing ourselves speak. Only when one is self-conscious is there reliable memory; this is not to say we don't forget—forget far more than we remember—but the forgotten time is not a dark hole, as it was for me in the intervals between my few memories. And sometimes the right clues can summon up a forgotten item. But I am sure that nothing will bring back my dark lost time.

At some moment as I moved between unconsciousness—although I was not formally comatose anymore, I cannot call my state mere sleep—and consciousness, I saw the inside of the top of my brain and understood that I was moving from one state to another and that the second state involved self-consciousness. I saw these states as if they had material being. It was an extraordinary sensation, one that aroused wonder in me even as I felt it, and for a second or two after I awoke, I remembered it. I retain some kind of visual trace memory of it still, but it is fading.

Another event I do not remember is a visit by Bella Abzug on the same day the coven (and others) visited. Apparently, I said, "Hello Bella!" with great pleasure but did not even greet my coven sisters. They reproach me for that to this day. They laugh, but they bring it up so often, and so reprovingly, that I know I committed a major sin. But what can I do? I have told them that they are family, and family doesn't warrant a special hello, whereas Bella was a guest, and did. I have told them that Bella was a major figure from my younger years, when I followed her exploits in the newspapers, silently cheering her on, whereas I did not know about them until I was older. But whatever I say cuts no ice with these unforgiving dames, who insist that I betrayed my preference for Bella over them—although I love them profoundly. They enjoy torturing me with it. Bella, of course, knows nothing about it.

Soon after this, I was moved to a private room upstairs, with round-the-clock nurses the children had hired. It was on my second or third night upstairs that I fell out of bed. At this time, I was still not conscious, or at least I have no memory of days or nights, remembering only moments. After I was moved upstairs, the regular morning visits began in which the doctors asked me where I was and what year it was. I didn't really care about the date but I remember giving the question of where I was great thought. I knew, with certainty, that I was north, that is, north of my apartment, perhaps in the Bronx or White Plains. I finally answered Yonkers. I don't know what symbolic value north has for me (Memorial Sloan-Kettering was actually south of my then apartment) or why I thought I'd gone in that direction. At least I didn't think I'd gone west.

Rob recalls me lying there silent, refusing to answer the doctors; he thought I was unwilling to admit I didn't know. He was probably right. But even after I was able to answer, he remained worried about me. Jamie and Barbara, who are both optimists as a rule, simply assumed I would be all right. But Rob, more pessimistic, was gripped by a new anxiety. The doctors had warned that I might have suffered brain damage during the seizures. They had warned that if I did wake up, if I did not have cancer of the brain, I might be an idiot, or might not be able to speak: nothing could be predicted. Each day after the doctors left, following their interrogation, the children would again explain to me where I was and what year it was. My inability the next day to remember these things suggested that my brain had indeed been damaged. Thus, Barbara's cheer when I announced that Clinton was President. Rob continued to worry for months, even after I slowly regained old abilities. Not until April, when I began to revise *Our Father* for the final time, was he sure that I would recover completely. (In fact, I do not believe I recovered completely, but I think what I lost was brain speed, not depth. It is probably difficult, though, to assess one's own loss of intellect.)

I did not hold on to much. They told me I'd been in a coma. Sometimes I understood that. Finally, I asked them to bring in a calendar, a big one, and mark the days I'd been comatose. Maybe visual evidence would impress it on my brain. They pasted a calendar to my tray table, but each time I glanced at it, it seemed new to me. It remained incomprehensible for a long time. Even after I could retain the words and could parrot, "I was in a coma for about two weeks," I did not comprehend what I said. Nor do I know how to explain my lack of comprehension. I knew the facts, but I had no experience of them. I was like a child who learns a multiplication table by rote; I could say 49-56-63 without having any notion of what actually constituted 49 or 56 or 63 of anything, or what their relation was to 7.

I did not think much about this; I noted it and waited for it to pass. I did not feel anything. I did not want to feel. I was afraid I would go to pieces. For my situation was dismal. I was helpless; like a tiny infant, I could not hold my head upright on my shoulders. I could not sit up by myself; each time I tried, a nurse would run over and pull me up. She would have to do this every half hour or so, because I kept sliding down, having no muscles to hold myself erect in the bed. Not only could I not get out of bed, but I could not lower myself to the toilet: a nurse had to sit me down and help me up. The bewilderment I felt about this humiliation (no one explained), and the quiet hysteria building in me from fear and confusion, converged into rage about the most utter helplessness I had ever felt. I had hated being a child because I hated being dependent; now I was more dependent than a three-year-old, and I did not understand why. The kids probably explained to me that muscles atrophy when they are not used, that Charlotte had urged the nurses to move my arms and legs while I was comatose, but I was hooked up to too many lines and connections to make moving my limbs feasible. Besides, of course, everyone expected me to die. But if an explanation was given, it did not sink in; I could not hold on to it, either.

Beyond that, my esophagus was a mass of ulcerations, and even drinking water caused me agonizing pain. I had a constant hard itching across my back, which frequent back rubs by the nurses did not relieve. Between the pain, the helplessness, and the lack of any other ability, my soul was in despair, but I did not allow myself to feel that. Though despair lay under everything, I never let it erupt into my surface life. What I did was sleep, as much as I could. I did not really want to see people or talk; I wanted to escape.

I was so sunk inward that I did not even think about my children. It was clear that they didn't go to work—they were at the hospital every day—but I never asked how they were surviving or whether their jobs were in danger. Nor did it occur to me to ask how they had paid for the ambulance, or who was paying the nurses—although the money would have had to come from them. Jamie, who worked for Outward Bound, told me recently that she really did not function in this period, and because she wasn't working, she just kept taking money out of the bank. In time, of course, she must have run out. I imagine the same happened to Rob, who held two jobs, working with language and computers at (then) Bell Labs and teaching linguistics at NYU. Barbara, who was going to school, had part-time jobs, but these could not keep them afloat. None of them ever complained or indicated to me in any way that they had problems. And somehow they survived, without any help from me.

By this time, all my veins were blown. I needed a port. (I kept remembering Roz fingering hers, saying, "At least I have my port," as one might say, "At least I have my Star of David," or my cross, or talisman, or eagle feather.) But I did not want a port, and the nurses discouraged me, saying they became infected and caused more problems than they were worth. Yet there were no veins left in my arms that could take an IV. (After a few days, four at most, a new site must be found for an IV. My veins had been used so often that they were flattened; the minute a needle entered them, they burst. The IV nurse had to puncture me again and again, searching for a vein that would hold. This situation has continued; I don't know how long it takes veins to regenerate, but all my more recent hospitalizations have been terminated prematurely because my veins could no longer hold an IV.)

At S-K, they could not send me home, and even the doctors only halfheartedly urged a port on me. Finally, lacking an arm vein, they put the IV in my foot. But the veins in the feet are tiny and the needle hurts; also, because I could not keep my legs still, the needle kept popping out. Each time this happened they had to start a new IV. Nurses and doctors reprimanded me several times a day, urging me to keep my leg still. When I told them I couldn't, they did not believe me. I have since found out that certain kidney problems can cause uncontrollable leg movements, but even the kind kidney specialist did not know about it when I thought to ask him. My constant movement was particularly damaging during dialysis. I underwent dialysis twice after I regained consciousness (or so I believe; the first time I was only half-conscious). During the second procedure, the leg movements had begun, and the exasperated technician said they had wrecked the treatment. However hard I tried, I could not keep my leg still. I found dialysis horrible, perhaps partly because of this, and I determined that if I had to undergo it for the rest of my life, I would kill myself. At that point, my life had little to recommend it anyway. Helpless, in agony from my esophagus, and unable to read or write or even think, I had little reason to welcome a future.

When the delighted kidney specialist appeared and told me that he had decided I did not require dialysis, I was tremendously relieved and in some way turned around. He gave me a reason, not to live, but at least not to die. I took a deep breath and began to think more positively. I asked the kids to resume daily delivery of the *New York Times*. But that led only to a fresh hell, as I discovered the next morning that I *could not read.* The letters shuddered under my eyes; I could not make them out. Appalled, I said nothing. My brain had been damaged, I decided. In a state of utter dread, I remembered my alternative: if I could no longer read or write, there was no question: I would kill myself. It did not occur to me to question my eyesight; after all, only two weeks before, I had read easily with my reading glasses.

Finally, I meekly brought up my difficulty with a doctor, who said eyes are sometimes affected by a coma.

Indeed, an S-K eye doctor said I just needed a new prescription for reading glasses. Like my hearing, my eyesight had declined another level; I might be sixty-two years old, but my body was now five or ten years older. With the new glasses, purchased as swiftly as Isabelle could manage, I could read! No brain damage after all. But I could not concentrate well enough to do the Sunday crossword puzzle.

Perhaps a week or ten days after I was moved upstairs, the hospital sent around a physical therapist, who worked with me for about twenty minutes several times a week. She was young, efficient, and mechanical; she made no personal connection with her patients—not at least with me—and had no affect whatever. I am sure that to her I was just one more helpless elderly woman, but I have since met so many warm, devoted, caring physiotherapists that I wonder if she was in the wrong field. Still, she did her job. She urged me to walk holding on to a walker. Hating this, I preferred to walk alongside my wheelchair, supported by it, while my nurse or one of the kids (usually Jamie) pushed it down the hospital corridor. The corridor paralleled the outside of the building, dividing the bedrooms, which were on the outside wall, from the nurses' stations and doctors' rooms and the kitchen and toilets and other facilities in the windowless core of the building. There were shortcuts through the core, but we rarely took them. The walk around the perimeter was too long for me at first; when I tired, I would sit in the wheelchair and be pushed back.

One day, Rob showed up with a pair of purple-blue high-tops, and I burst out laughing. The style was appropriate for a three-year-old, I said, and since that was a little beyond my present skills in walking, the shoes would be something to grow into. He was right in his choice, though; I walked much better in those shoes than I did in slippers or the low-heeled pumps I had asked Isabelle to bring in for me. Grotesque as they are to my eye, I still wear them on days when I am going to do something tiring, like visit a museum.

Hooked up to an IV, I was being fed that way, since swallowing was intolerable. But the doctors began urging me to eat. I thought they were mad or callous. Did they have any idea how I felt? They explained that I could probably now go home, but not until I could maintain myself off the IV. That meant I had to eat. After a few days, I understood what they were saying. If they had couched it in reasonable terms from the beginning, instead of uttering it as a threat, I might have understood sooner. But perhaps not. My understanding was not great. By now, they had weaned me off Dilantin but were giving me phenobarbital, and the room often whirled around me as I sat there, largely because of this drug. I also took ulcer medications, and perhaps some others I don't recall.

I wanted to go home, of course. But I could not get food down my gullet. It was entirely too painful. So I began to drink the enriched protein drinks that come in cans. These had been offered to me earlier, when I was starving after the radiation, but I loathed them too much to drink them. An American invention, they of course are loaded with sugar, typical of a nation that puts sugar in baby food, commercial salad dressing, and even toothpaste. I had strongly disliked sugar from my late teens and used it only in iced tea (which I rarely drank) and the vinegar in which I marinate cucumbers. But now I loaded a glass with ice, held my nose, and drank the damned stuff. I found the chocolate flavor the least plastic-tasting and could tolerate it if it was icy cold. I was a stick when I began, but I boasted to the doctors that I was gaining weight. The nurses who weighed me every couple of days confirmed this. I don't recall what I weighed then, but it was too little for a person of my height and bone structure. When I got up to about 110, still very thin for me, they said I could go home. But this time I did not look forward to home-coming with joy, with faith that I was going to recover my strength and resume my old life. I wanted to go home because I was more comfortable there, and I had access to my things, and I hate hospital beds. But I had nothing else to look forward to.

1993

FEBRUARY—APRIL

I was released from Sloan-Kettering for the last time on February 4, 1993. I have returned since only for day treatments—endoscopies, which I needed often in the years following my treatment—or to consult my neurologist or oncologist.

I went home. The children hired the same nurses who had tended me in the hospital—Ursula, Gay, and Yvonne. In hospital, I loved Ursula best; outspoken and forceful, she cared for me almost affectionately. But she behaved differently in my house, perhaps put off by a penthouse duplex with terraces overlooking Central Park. For whatever reason, she became sullen and opportunistic, attitudes that intensified gradually as I needed her less. Ursula, originally from Guyana, was married, with a teenage son and a younger daughter, but she never spoke of her husband, and rarely of her son. I had the feeling she had given up on them, but her daughter was central in her life. The girl was bright and talented, and Ursula was as ambitious for her as she was for herself. Like the other nurses, she was a student working toward an R.N. degree, and between chores, she pored over her texts. She was very intelligent and made high grades.

Gay, too, was from Guyana, but she had a very different nature. A late child in a large family, she was taken in after her parents died by siblings who treated her like a slave. She was not allowed to leave for school in the morning until she had put in several hours of work; her life was made hard in every possible way. Younger than my other nurses, she was a meek woman, whose pious servility I at first disliked. But as she came to trust me and tell me her story, I began to understand her manner and grew to like her very much.

Gay was married to a young man she regarded as her savior: loving her, he had "saved" her from her sister's brutality and meanness. That alone made him her hero. Then he brought her to the United States and "allowed" her to attend nursing school. Her husband, however, was not essentially different from her sister, except that he used love rather than cruelty to enforce his will. Since she worked as a home nursing aide, she often had to spend evenings away, but he refused to eat if she did not prepare his meal for him. If she had to stay out late she had to prepare his dinner early in the morning, before work and her classes; and she could never go on a trip. He was helpless, incapable of using a dustcloth or a vacuum or running a washing machine, so in addition to working eight hours a day for me or another patient, going to school, and studying, she had to do everything in the house, walking long blocks (he of course took the car; conveniently, she could not drive) carrying heavy loads to the laundromat and from the supermarket.

There were other problems, but when I suggested she could solve them by negotiating with him, she demurred ever so sweetly. She loved him so much, she said, she didn't like to upset him: he just *couldn't* do this or that. I forbore to point out that she had exchanged one dictator for another. I knew she would discover this in time, when his behavior grew even more oppressive—as such behavior always does when unchecked.

It was Gay who had been supposed to be with me the night I fell out of bed, and for some reason, every time I fell down (as I did several times in the early months: one minute I'd be standing, the next I'd be on the floor), Gay was caring for me. This upset her horribly. Once, she cried out near tears, "You always fall when I'm with you!" as if some doom attended our connection.

Yvonne became my favorite. She was the one the kids had first approached, who had mustered the others to take care of me. An energetic person, enterprising and confident, she had been with me the first night after I left the SCU, a terrible night, she said. Unconscious, I was restless and in pain, constantly tossing and turning, and she had had to change my sheets and clean me up six times during the night. I had little memory of her in the hospital, because she was on duty mainly at night. She usually took night duty at my house, too (although she and Ursula sometimes switched shifts). She would prepare me for bed—standing beside me at the sink (lest I fall down), squeezing the toothpaste out of the tube for me (I could not even do that!)—and be there in the night. The nurses slept in my room on a fold-out bed. I was not supposed to get up without their help but was to call them—and keep calling them until they woke (which I was reluctant to do until my first fall).

Every night, when Yvonne came into my room, I would ask her what she'd done all day, and what her father-in-law had made for dinner, and how her little girl was, and what her husband was doing. I was interested in the lives of all three women who tended me, but Gay's stories distressed me and Ursula's rare references to her domestic life crackled with concealed bitterness and rage. Only her daughter and nursing made her happy—and getting good grades.

But Yvonne had been praised all her life. She was a loved child, and to those who are given, more is given: children lucky enough to be loved usually grow up into loving—and loved—adults. She was a lighthearted person, very smart and ambitious; her family was prominent in Haiti, but she had left, fearing the secret military force that had succeeded the Tontons Macoutes. In college in Haiti, she had majored in economics, but her highly intelligent Haitian husband, whom she had married in the United States, had persuaded her to give up the idea of an academic career for one in nursing. I didn't know whether she was realistic in looking up to her husband's intellect as she did, but his role in forging her future seemed suspect to me. Nursing is much harder work than teaching economics and has less prestige—but it pays better, at least at first. On the other hand, as a nonwhite foreigner, it is possible that Yvonne would have encountered severe barriers in an exalted academic field, and her husband may have known that.

She had had a child about five years before, and her husband was totally enamored of the little girl. Yvonne, too, adored her daughter, but she was jealous of her husband's affection for the child. In speaking of this, she was very funny—not the least guilt-ridden about her jealousy (as most middle-class white American women would be) nor at all resentful of her daughter because her father gave her more love than he gave Yvonne (as many women would be). But as a result of his behavior, she adamantly, steadfastly refused to have another child. Like Ursula's and Gay's husbands, Yvonne's husband would not help around the house. (I often say that the only creature in the entire animal kingdom who can't take care of himself is the human male.) Yvonne worked harder than he: he was a welfare officer of some sort and worked an eight-hour day; she worked an eight-hour day (or night), went to school, studied, and did the housework and cooking and child care. When she complained, her husband sent for his father in Haiti. A wonderful cook and a meticulous housekeeper (as was Yvonne), who loved Yvonne and his grandchild and being with them, he made their lives a pleasure. Like Gay, Yvonne held nothing against her husband and was on the whole a happy woman.

Bright and ambitious, like Ursula, Yvonne worked hard and made good grades at school. Her tales of her busy days, the delicious and (to me) unusual meals her father-in-law cooked each night, and her adorable daughter's doings calmed me as I faced going to sleep. Filled with joy and humor, like Yvonne herself, her stories were so ordinary, so quotidian, that they made me forget my situation.

My situation was grim. I remained on phenobarbital and was not able to stop taking it for fear of inducing the brain seizures it had been prescribed to control. The drug made me drowsy all day long, and dizzy as well: the room where I sat was frequently in motion. I still could not eat, but lived on Ensure with lots of ice, chilled watermelon, and Italian ices. I drank aloe vera, water, and herbal tea. I longed for carbonated drinks like seltzer or ginger ale, but they touched off agonizing currents in my esophagus. I thought then it was because of the ulcerations, but the ulcerations are gone now, and carbonated drinks still cause me extreme pain. Nor could I move alone, because of my weak muscles and dizziness; I needed help to do anything.

Beyond that, I was in a state of grief. This was a non-specific emotion: I was grieving for myself, for what had happened to me. I had been traumatized by the events of the last months, although that word never entered my mind. Nor did I think about what was going on in my life (most unusual for me). I simply grieved.

A week after my release, a physical therapist came to me, sent by the hospital. Michael was militantly cheerful and personally seductive; he employed charm to keep his patients, especially elderly women. But I did not dislike him: his style was more agreeable than the mechanical style of the therapist in the hospital. He started me on exercises to help me regain muscle strength and enlisted Gay (who usually chose day duty, since she had to be home at night to feed her helpless mate) to make sure I did them twice every day, morning and night, with the number of repetitions he had ordered. He liked to give orders and tried to set up a hierarchy of command from him to Gay to me. Gay was of course compliant in this—as she would be in any tyranny. (Sad to say, the gentle Gays of the world can easily become dictators' minions.) But I found it absurd. I did the exercises faithfully because I wanted to get stronger, not because Michael had ordered them or because Gay was counting. But I did them only once a day, in the morning. My noncomplicity in the emotions of the pecking order quickly ended Michael's efforts at establishing a little kingdom in my house; I never had to frown, much less complain about it.

That same day, I had an appointment with my oncologist at S-K. Getting there was a major enterprise: Ursula and Isabelle put on their coats, scarves, and hats, bundled me up in a warm coat and the rest, assisted me into the elevator; I waited indoors, in the lobby, where I could be warm and sit down, while Isabelle and the doorman went outdoors and hailed a cab. When it arrived, I started outside. Isabelle opened the cab door, and she and Ursula helped me inside it. At the hospital, a doorman opened the cab door; Isabelle paid the driver and then helped me out, while Ursula went indoors and fetched a wheelchair. She wheeled me into the elevator and up to the fourth floor, Isabelle trailing alongside. I felt like a crone of ninety or more, slumped over in my seat (I still could not sit up straight), utterly helpless.

Although I had said nothing about it, and had con-cealed it even from myself, I was in a fury, and it all came pouring out onto my oncologist during that first visit. I was furious with *him,* quite apart from my con-dition. Upset by his negativity about the disappearance of the tumor, I was appalled that he had not visited me once during the times when I was hospitalized with fever, had come only once when I was in the coma, and then had not sought out my children. He had never once visited me during the four weeks after I woke from the coma; Bruce Minsky did, as did the sweet urologist whose name I did not know. I did not see why I should regard him as "my" doctor. That we had to wait quite a while before they wheeled me into his office only stoked my anger. By the time he entered, I was beside myself.

"I don't know what I'm doing here!" I said, in a low, furious voice. "I should be seeing Dr. Kevorkian, not you!"

He turned swiftly to his nurse. "Call Psychiatry!" he cried in alarm.

"Why did you bother keeping me alive to leave me in this shape?" I continued.

But he was not about to deal with this crazy woman—as I suppose he saw it. He didn't know me, had never known me, and was not interested in know-ing me. He had his nurse usher me out of his office to another waiting room, to see a psychiatrist.

The psychiatrist, a woman in her late fifties or early sixties, was no more interested in me than he was. She asked me a few perfunctory questions, which I answered with equal shortness and considerable quiet rage.

"You'll have to come back," she said coldly.

"The hell I will," I said with equal coldness. "You can't help me."

This first visit to S-K after my release marked a change in me as a patient. I was no doubt unfair to the oncologist (but not to the bored, superior psychiatrist) in blaming him for my state, but I had good reason to be furious with a medical establishment that had rendered me utterly helpless without ever trying to offer any explanation for the coma or my present state, any prognosis for my recovery, or any overview of my condition. It was after all, I thought then, the treatment they gave me that had caused my coma—iatrogenic, it had almost killed me. A simple apology would have been nice; an explanation of things would have been better. But I suppose they would have seen an apology as a possible admission of guilt, grounds for a lawsuit. Still, a doctor with even rudimentary empathy would have understood my terror and rage at the trauma of coma and of waking helpless. My oncologist's terrified cry for "Psychiatry" only increased my contempt for him. Perhaps he feared I would attack him—how, given my physical weakness, I have no idea. The man was so out of things that on my next visit, he asked me why I couldn't walk.

"*You* tell *me*!" I exploded. "Aren't you the doctor?"

I never forgave him for any of these things, perhaps because I never told him why I was angry with him. I would not make that mistake with other doctors. My future dealings with the medical establishment were of another order of control and suspicion.

*

My daily routine in these months was as follows: A nurse would wake me about eleven, help me up to wash, then help me get back in bed and drink the tea she had brought me. Before the coma, I had drunk orange juice in the morning, but my throat could not tolerate acidic drinks now. Sometimes she brought me icy aloe vera, which was calming.

I would read the first section of the *New York Times* while I had my drink. Afterward, I did my exercises (which became more complicated and lengthy as time went on); the nurse watched, helping me count. Bathing was fraught, for both me and my nurse. I was so fragile and so bony and weak that getting into the tub was a major production. The nurse would draw the bath, then help me to step into it, holding on to me as well as she could. Sitting down was the most terrifying part, as she could not get a good purchase on me from outside the tub, and I had little control over my leg muscles. When it started to grow back, in March, I had to wash my hair in the tub, as standing under a shower was still too dangerous—I might fall at any moment, and the nurse could not get into my stall shower with me. I would wash it in the tub water and Gay (or Ursula) would rinse it with clean water poured from a pitcher.

The nurse helped me to dress. The first step was a light massage of most of my body, using a scented lotion or cream she heated in a basin of hot water beforehand. I thought this was designed primarily to make me feel better; I did not realize how wrinkled and dry my body was: I barely looked at it. The nurse would take from my closet whatever I pointed to, or some-times she would pull out something that appealed to her. As I had when I was undergoing chemo, I wore pants and a sweater every day, but my clothes swam on me, which made dressing disheartening.

Then I would make my way proudly downstairs by myself—going up and down stairs (holding on to the banister) was the one thing I could always manage, for some reason—and lie on the couch in my study, gazing out at the park, and finish the newspaper. When I was not reading the paper, I was sleeping. I did not read anything else, nor did I write. I slept a great deal. I was always tired from the drugs and the whirling of the room. After the first month, I would move from room to room with a cane, practicing walking. I'd gaze out the window, examining the snowed-in cars or the bare branches of the trees or, later, the beginnings of buds. But nothing I saw aroused any emotion. The nurses were right behind me, or at my elbow, ready to grab me if I started to fall. But no care really could prevent it when it happened: I just went down. For some reason, I always fell in the bathroom, with its tile floor (most of the apartment was carpeted). And during the time I had nurses, I always fell when Gay was with me. I doubt there was any significance to that; after the nurses were gone, I still fell, usually in the morning and in the bath- room.

Lunch was usually an iced chocolate Ensure, with ice-cold watermelon or an Italian ice. After lunch I would usually nap. Guests came in the afternoons and early evenings. When I had no guests and was awake, I listened to Mozart on the CD player the kids had bought me, or to WNYC. I still could not tolerate tele- vision. Dinner was the same as lunch, I think—I have little recall of meals during this period. I know I suggested a few things—scrambled or boiled eggs and various soups, for instance—only to discover I could not get them down.

Michael came three times a week; other practitioners also visited, including a doctor sent by Gloria, who had helped her change her diet after her bout with breast cancer. Sandra McLanahan, an M.D. who prescribes only natural medicines, suggested I follow a modified macrobiotic diet and prescribed, among other things, a tea of comfrey and chamomile to be drunk every other day. This proved to be the most calming and quieting drink I had ever taken.

On morning soon after I arrived home, I awoke to a new horror: I could barely move my left arm or either of my hands. Overnight, I had developed arthritis. I could no longer pour myself a glass of water, something I had been able to do for only a little over a week. It was too much. I nearly collapsed, feeling like someone who had fought off the onslaught of the ocean and managed to swim in close to shore, then was overwhelmed by a sudden giant wave. Helplessness heaped on helplessness. When I spoke to friends of the arthritis, I nearly cried.

In early March, guests' names begin to appear on my calendar: I'd had appointments with visitors before that but had not asked Isabelle to record their names. The children, whose names are not noted, were with me much of the time. I went out only to doctors' offices. During my first angry visit, the oncologist had told Isabelle to make another appointment for me a month hence. I had asked him to stop the phenobarbital, so he told me to have an EEG to check for brain damage, and to see a neuro-oncologist at S-K.

I had the EEG the next week and saw the neurologist two weeks later. At first, this man struck me as bordering on crazy, because as he read my records (from a then four-foot-high file), he continually hummed under his breath and occasionally davened.

He said, "Oh, you're a writer. Doctors hate writers; they always say horrible things about us." He told me his wife knew my work, and asked if I would autograph a book next time I came. I said I would. He said he thought I was a person of spirit—was that true? I said I hoped so. He said, "I was afraid of that."

"You don't like people of spirit?"

"Not women," he said calmly.

He wore a yarmulke, and I imagined his wife wore a wig or a kerchief and was forbidden to act on her own. But such a woman would be most unlikely to have read *The Women's Room*. He also seemed too intelligent to have a meek, submissive wife. And aside from his humming and davening, he appeared too calm and contained and, somehow, *amused,* ironic, to oppress anyone. In the end, I found him a lovable man, intelligent and thoughtful. He was keenly aware of the limitations of medical knowledge and treated me with care.

My EEG showed considerable disturbance, but he was not sure whether this was brain damage or a result of the phenobarbital. I knew the drug helped me sleep, which I liked (having before my illness often suffered from insomnia), but I believed it caused the continual circulation of the world around me, which I wanted to stop. He drew up a schedule, graduating my dosage. I complained of having little feeling in my toes; he tested me, then said I had peripheral neuropathy, a common result of chemotherapy, and that it might get worse. It did.

On March 11, I saw the oncologist again. This was the visit during which he asked me why I could not walk. I felt he was just marking time with me until the tumor reappeared. He told me that when—if—it did, there was nothing more he could do for me. He prescribed pills for the arthritis but had no answer when I asked why it had come upon me just then. I felt unmoored in a sea of uncertainty. No one was taking care of my whole self. I felt that if no one saw me whole, no one could help me. Each doctor cared only about his specialty: the oncologist cared only about cancer, the neuro-oncologist only about nerve damage caused by cancer. I had not yet reached the point of doing something about this, taking my fate in my own hands.

I had been listening to the news on WNYC, following the events at Waco with a sinking heart, when I heard, on February 28, that the ATF and the FBI had surrounded the Branch Davidian compound. I cried out so loudly that the nurse came running into the room. In that instant, I knew that disaster was inevitable, that the impasse would end in some kind of fiery cataclysm—probably a shoot-out, with automatic weapons on both sides. For both sides were the same. I sympathize with those who blame the government for Waco, because it was totally unnecessary. The approach the government took was confrontational, seeking war, not negotiation. There was no need to surround the compound. Whatever was going on there could have been ended in a peaceable way. But the groups that blame the government think just like the government: it is showdown time, for all of them. Davidians, Christian militias, the government, all think alike, and the way they think—or rather feel, for very little logical reason informs their decisions— is what we have come to call macho: a mindless drive to impress with strength of muscle or firepower, a need to force an "enemy" to bow, a desperate need to prove one's "manliness." The ending of the Davidians was implicit that day and, for me, was never in question afterward, although it made me weep.

Barbara Greenberg came down from Boston to visit, and I asked her to promise me that if I was again in a dire condition, she would help me kill myself. She said she would in some hypothetical future, but definitely not now. She did not know, any more than anyone else, whether I would recover from my present state, but she had a more positive outlook than my doctors. I don't know why in this period I fixated on suicide when I was with close friends. I never thought about it when I was alone, but when I was with intimates (not my children, though), I could speak of little else. It was as if I was trying to avoid my present state, a little after the fact.

The arthritis pills proved useless, so I made an appointment with a rheumatologist recommended by the oncologist. His office was near S-K, and I saw him the following week. All these visits were ordeals: the nurse would bundle me up, there was the rigmarole of hailing a cab, getting in and out of it, getting to the doctor's office, undressing there while being supported by my nurse, then being dressed again and propped in a chair to hear the verdict. This examination was painful, because I had to lie nearly naked on a hard, narrow table to be X-rayed. The cold metal table pressed painfully into the now-protruding knobs of my spine. When the doctor announced that he would inject cortisone in my shoulder joint, I heard myself ask if it would hurt. Suddenly, I was aware that my entire physical disposition had changed. I had always been a stoic patient. For example, although I had had huge cavities as a young woman, I always refused Novocain, preferring the brief pain of the dental drill to the soreness and swelling of the anesthetic for the rest of the day. I had never shrunk from pain, never even thought about it. I had not feared pain.

But now I felt my body physically shrink away from the rheumatologist and his needle; I almost whimpered. My body bore a memory of pain that would be indelible.

I could not take ibuprofen, which helps many arthritis sufferers, because of its effect on the digestive system: mine now opened into ulcers at the slightest provocation. And the cortisone helped not at all. Even before he knew this, however, the rheumatologist prescribed steroids. I said I would not take them. He said I had to, they were the only medication that would help, that all his patients took them and got better. I refused and left. Later, I told the oncologist that the rheumatologist he recommended was a drug pusher and should be stopped.

Isabelle found me an acupuncturist. Elizabeth Call was a lovely young woman, and I was amazed by her demonstrations of the connections among body parts. She would push a finger in my torso near the belly and ask, "Does that hurt?" It did. Then, with one hand, she would press a spot on my foot and, with the other, press the spot near my belly again. "Now does it hurt?" It did not. Such connections seem to exist all over the body; the torso seems most profoundly related to the feet. I know various religions and medical systems use this connection symbolically, but I ponder its nonreligious meaning. Why the feet? After all, the way humans use feet is one of the latest adaptations our bodies made. That we put our entire weight on two feet, walking upright, is not a five-million-year-old development, like, say, the reptile brain, but more like a three-and-a-half-million-year-old one. So why should feet bear such significance? It's interesting. Still, the acupuncture did not relieve the arthritis at all, which disappointed me greatly. Thinking it might be a painless way out, I agreed to a course of treatment, because I wanted it to work; I would give it a chance.

At the end of that week, the coven met at my house. I had the dinner catered by the same woman who'd prepared the food the disastrous night of the fire, and I managed to sit up at the table for most of the meal, if not to eat it. But after dinner, as we sat in my study, I reproached my friends. They were all sitting on the couch with me, touching me. I was crying. It is the only time I remember crying, at home or in hospital, in the post-coma period. I don't recall giving them the details of my physical debility; perhaps I did, but I probably didn't need to: they could see with their own eyes the wrinkled shell of a person, frail and shriveled and unable to sit up, walk, stand from a sitting position, or even sit down unaided; unable to use one arm or do much with either hand; unable to eat solid food or concentrate or find a peaceful, still space in any room. I blamed my condition on them.

"You kept me alive!" I raged. "What for! Why did you do it? Look at me now!"

By now they were crying too.

"Oh, bubby, we want you alive," Esther wept.

Carol kept hugging me, tears on her cheeks.

"You know what we did? We made the same mistake people always make, Marilyn," said Gloria. "We did what *we* wanted, assuming that's what you'd want, never thinking what you might want. We're sorry. But you know, we could always feel you present. I thought you didn't want to go." Gloria is always rational, always able to see the other person's position. Blubbering, I hugged them and apologized for blaming them for what was, after all, not utterly in their control. They had no doubt helped to keep me alive, but divine as they are, they are not divinities. My kids were just as responsible, but I never uttered a word of blame to them. I guess I was taking things out on the tough ones.

I told them I wanted to die, and they were appalled. Carol, especially, could not understand this then— although I think she does now. I asked them to kill me if I got sick again, and they turned a little green. They did not want to talk about this, and I did not pursue the subject.

During this period, I had thoughts and impressions, but my second brain, the one that is always conscious of what the first one is doing, was not working well. I had had a second brain since about the age of four, and at brief moments before that. It kept track of what I said and did and felt; it remembered, it paid attention and sent me messages that I had just sounded angry, or that what I was saying was offending someone, or that I had been crying a lot lately. I have referred earlier to this self-consciousness; I believe that much behavior and speech and emotion is largely unselfconscious—transient and without larger meaning to the self. I also think that people who were exposed to the ideas of Freud have a greater degree of this self-consciousness than those who were not. If you have aged relatives or friends, you perhaps have noted how direct and unself-conscious their behavior is.

I realize now that I considered suicide daily during this period. I had considered it several times in my life—in my childhood and again in my late twenties. For about a year—until I became tough—it was the only way I could imagine to get out of a hellish marriage. The sense of lacking alternatives that oppressed me then oppressed me now, and in the months after waking from the coma, I had to make a choice literally daily about whether I wanted to continue living a life that was essentially unbearable. When life is unbearable, one needs to own the alternative of *not* living. The idea of dying puts life in perspective, provides a needed balance. Killing oneself is so extreme an act that continuing to live seems easier. But knowing there is a way out helps you stay sane and enables you to face each day as a positive choice.

I made no move to kill myself—I did not at that time have the means to encompass suicide—nor did I think about finding any. Suicide was just there, in the back of my mind, as a talisman, a safety valve, a last resort. It may be a basic human way of surviving: I think of the various Beckett characters who say, "I won't go on, I can't go on, I'll go on."

My negotiations with myself continued until I was stronger and no longer needed the alternative of death to make life seem a positive course. I probably upset people with my talk, but it was necessary to me.

In mid-March, my calendar becomes crowded, mainly with doctors' appointments, but also with visits by friends and business associates—my publisher, Jim Silberman; my accountant, Arthur Greene; and my investment counselor, Bill Reik. The *business* of life was resuming after nearly a year. Sometime near the end of March, I began the final revision of *Our Father*. My hands could not type, and I could not sit erect, so Isabelle sat at the computer, across from me, typing in the corrections and changes I read out to her from copy I'd edited with a pencil as I leaned back on the couch. It went slowly. I found I had omitted an entire chapter when I sent the manuscript to Jim; I had written the chapter in the hospital, on my laptop, and never transferred it to my hard disk. I found it ironic that I had written a novel in which a man lies in a coma, hovering between life and death, an experience I had not had when I conceived the story. It is not the first time that my writing foreshadowed an event or an object in my life.

By early April, the acupuncturist, realizing she was not helping me, said I should stop the treatments. I would have continued, on the off-chance of an eventual effect, and I was grateful for her honesty and responsibility. Michael, my physiotherapist, brought in an electrical acupuncture machine and gave me a treatment. It relieved me a little, but very little. Michael said he could help me regain the use of my arm and hands by forcibly breaking down the adhesions that were paralyzing me. The problem was it would be painful. "Do it," I said.

After that, the major part of his hour with me was devoted to exercises to increase my strength, followed by a short period—all I could stand—of "torture time," as I called it. Michael would bend a joint as far as he could; you could hear the cracking of the adhesion. Once the agonizing pain subsided, I could move the joint a bit more than before. This had to be done with each of the three finger joints, the wrist joints forward and backward, and elbow and shoulder joints in several directions. Michael worked on only a couple of joints a session; it took months to cover the entire affected area. He also gave me exercises to maintain flexibility. By May, I could move my arm and hands, although I continued exercises and heat treatments with a Hydrocollator almost until the end of the year. It had been painful, but by August I was fairly normal again, and I'd done it without steroids.

Michael began taking me out for walks once or

twice a week. We'd stroll down Central Park West—he liked to pass the El Dorado, hoping to catch a glimpse of Michael J. Fox, who lived there. We never covered more than ten blocks: five down, five back, short numbered blocks. For some reason, walking across town was harder for me: I think there may have been a slight incline going west. The long block to Columbus was the equivalent of three of the short ones; then we would go down a block, then return. I preferred walking along the park, where there were benches in case I tired (as I usually did).

The kids took me up and down Central Park West whenever they came, insisting I put on my purple high-tops, making sure I was dressed warmly, handing me my cane. I felt like an old lady out on a leash; God knows there were lots of old ladies being pushed in wheelchairs, usually by a home care worker, up and down the same street. But I gritted my teeth and went. Besides, I was happy when I was with my children, no matter what we were doing. On April 17, Jamie had come and made me dinner; she stayed overnight and the next day walked me to Columbus Avenue, where we had brunch in a restaurant. I have this Sunday circled on my calendar; it was my first time out without a nurse, my first walk without Michael, and my first meal in a restaurant since my return from the hospital. The only disappointment was that the Bloody Mary burned my throat and had to be forsaken, but even so, I was thrilled. Perhaps I would get better.

The nurses claimed I would.

1993

SPRING—SUMMER

During this period, no doctor even touched on the possibilities for my recovery; I was starved for an *informed* optimistic opinion. My children and my friends were encouraging, but hope offered by friends signified only goodwill. My three nurses were not as informed as doctors, but they were informed enough. They would do. I could believe them. Perhaps they did not fully understand the nature of esophageal cancer, but they had tended people awakening from comas. All three had done home nursing for many years to finance their education, and all three were generous. With each new accomplishment—a steadier gait, the ability to get up or sit down without their help (using my hands to support myself) or to sit erect in a chair for ten minutes—one of them would crow, "Look at you! You're doing great!" Then she would tell me about a patient—always younger than I (but some in comas for longer)—who did not manage that for four months or six, while I had done it in only two months or three. They usually compared me to younger men. They gave me hope and the will to go on doing exercises, no matter how painful or frustrating they might be. I bless them still. Michael, too, praised me continually, stating that women my age simply gave up and became invalids. This sounded like a stereotype, and I doubted it. But I could not challenge it.

The nurses assured me—and for months, I needed regular reassurance—that I *would* get better, that I did not have to remain a helpless lump for the rest of my days. It was their utter assurance that recovery was within the realm of possibility for someone like me that strengthened me. When they proclaimed (always with great authority) that I would recover, I would ask how long it would take. There the brows wrinkled, the hems and haws began. Well, this one took a year, that one a year plus, another guy took three years, she thought, though she did not work for him that long. But I was doing so well that who knew? Maybe even less than a year!

In fact, if nothing further had happened to me, I imagine it would have taken several years to recover from my injuries. In 1995, Jamie, crossing the street near her house, was hit by a cab speeding around the corner and hurled many yards. Unconscious, she came down on her back on the hard pavement. Luckily, it was deep winter and she was wearing a heavy coat and hat, and the only damage done was severed cartilage in her left knee. She required a transplant of cartilage from elsewhere in her leg to help repair the tear. She wore a leg brace and used crutches for months afterward and required almost a full year of physical therapy to regain ninety percent of her leg movement. If a torn cartilage takes a year, how long does a destroyed body take? But I did not yet know how destroyed my body was.

At the end of March, I had a CT scan of my throat and chest, which revealed no sign of cancer. My oncologist was unmoved in his pessimism, and I accepted that I would not live long, that the cancer was almost certain to recur. So I did not look forward. I did not think about the future. I made no plans. I held no hopes. I was a cripple with almost no physical powers, unsure that my mental powers were intact. All I could do was wait.

But looking back made me trembly and teary; looking back meant recalling the coma, and everything in me, mind and emotion, shrank from that. So I did not look back, either. I lived completely in the moment, which unfortunately was not wonderful. The ability to find bliss in the moment, which I had so carefully cultivated the year before, had vanished.

It is hard to describe my mental state in these months. I was not comatose, yet not in a state of mind that I recognize as fully conscious. I was flattened, insulated, numbed. Little penetrated my deadheadedness. I wanted mainly to sleep: I didn't care what I ate or wore or saw. Even listening to music merely filled time. I was not inside myself.

A few years later, when I tried to describe this mental state to Gloria, she recommended a book that might help, *Trauma and Recovery,* by Judith Lewis Herman (New York: Basic Books, 1992). The next day, she sent it to me. This book deals with serious trauma generated by combat, death camps, rape, and continued childhood sexual abuse. What I had suffered did not compare to these, but Herman's descriptions of trauma nevertheless describe my feelings as well. For instance, she writes: "Traumatic events violate the autonomy of the person at the level of basic bodily integrity. The body is invaded, injured, defiled. Control over bodily functions is often lost." Many people find this loss of control "the most humiliating aspect of the trauma" (pages 52–3). "Traumatic events appear to recondition the human nervous system" (36), leaving people with "an elevated baseline of arousal: their bodies are always on the alert for danger. They have . . . an intense reaction to specific stimuli associated with the traumatic event. After a traumatic experience, the human system of self-preservation seems to go onto permanent alert, as if the danger might return at any moment" (35). A state of "hyper-arousal is the first cardinal symptom of post-traumatic stress disorder" (35); "the traumatized person startles easily [and] reacts irritably to small provocations" (35).

For a couple of years after the coma, I was a pain in the neck in a car, crying out at the slightest provocation, terrifying the driver. I had never been like this before, nor could I control it, no matter how hard I tried. Also, I had a short fuse for frustration and exploded when things went wrong, especially when I was trying to manage on my own—to walk, shop, or deal commercially with others.

Herman cites Primo Levi, describing inmates of a death camp: "In the month of August, 1944, we who had entered the camp five months before now counted among the old ones. . . . Our wisdom lay in 'not trying to understand,' not imagining the future, not torment- ing ourselves as to how and when it would all be over, not asking others or ourselves any questions. . . . For living men, the units of time always have a value. For us, history had stopped" (89).*

My trauma was merely a bad dream compared to Levi's season in hell, yet I felt the same way. I ques- tioned nothing, wondered about nothing except the possibility of recovery, and expected nothing. Herman writes that children who are kidnapped and threatened with death retain a sense of futurelessness for years after the event: "when asked what they wanted to be when they grew up, many replied that they never fanta- sized or made plans for the future because they ex- pected to die young" (47).

Since "the core experiences of psychological trauma are disempowerment and disconnection from others," recovery requires renewed empowerment and the cre- ation of new connections (Herman, 134). For me, the essential step was reempowerment—the regaining of my physical abilities; I did not require new connec- tions. Except for when I was comatose, I had not lost the ability to enjoy my friends: Rob said that once I woke up, no one came to see me whom I did not rec- ognize and greet. I clutched that fact to me like a kind

*Primo Levi, *Survival in Auschwitz: The New Assault on Humanity* (1958), trans. Stuart Woolf (New York: Collier, 1961), 106–7.

of holy medal. Even if I did not remember their visits, I had been aware of my visitors' presence. That I was never out of contact with people seemed to me a sign of hope.

I felt better as I became able to do more things, and as that happened, I also took more pleasure in seeing people. My calendar suggests that by the second week of March, my spirits were rising; it is filled with notations of visits, not just by "family"—the kids and my closest pals—but by other old friends I treasure.

My visitors were the usual suspects, with some added treats. Chris Shepherd visited from London to weep with me. Barbara Raskin came from Washington, D.C., and Donna McKechnie came from California to advise me on arthritis. My former son-in-law, Bruce Gagnier, came to console me. Lisa Alther, on a trip down from Vermont, visited one afternoon, as did Alix Kates Shulman, Carolyn Heilbrun, Candace Hogan, and Wilbur Colom.

By the third week of April 1993, after almost three months of physiotherapy, I could walk, not very steadily or in a straight line (because of the chemotherapy-caused peripheral neuropathy in my feet and damage to the balance center of my brain), with a cane to support me in case I felt dizzy. I had regained movement in my left arm and my hands, although they had little strength; still, supporting myself with my arms, I could now lower myself into a chair and rise again. Sometimes, rising took several tries. The kids found it hilarious when I fell back down as I tried to rise, or walked in a circle right into a wall. Their laughter probably kept me from crying, which is what I felt like doing each time this happened. In my childhood, efficiency was considered essential in all endeavors. My family scorned sloppiness in thought or movement; they would have regarded with contempt one who continually dropped things (for the peripheral neuropathy had also affected my fingertips) or walked into walls. I did this even though my dose of phenobarbital was lower (it would end completely by late May).

I was able to swallow a few more foods—a few soups, applesauce, papaya, things soft and moist. I could not swallow any but the softest, gluiest glop, so I did not eat bread. Nor could I eat anything at all spicy, acid, or carbonated. But the pain of swallowing was largely gone.

Mother's Day, early in May, is not a major event in our family, because for years I derided it as it a commercial invention. Still, I have to admit with a certain chagrin that once the kids were grown and gone, a certain anxiety crept upon me each year as it approached lest they forget it. And some years, one of them did, which I, perversely, found hurtful. But they usually took me out for brunch—I had vetoed gifts. This year, I expected nothing. The children came to my apartment on Saturday night, made dinner, and stayed overnight. They said nothing about Sunday.

After eating breakfast, taking my medications, doing my exercises, bathing, and dressing, I came down about noon. The three kids were standing on the terrace outside my study; the door was open, and they smiled at me as I walked into the room. And then I saw the terrace was blooming from one end to another. They had planted every box, filled every pot, made the terrace gorgeous with flowers: lilies, pansies, petunias, marigolds, portulacas, and irises overflowed the boxes, scented the air. I was overwhelmed. Sitting me down on a cushioned chair, they sat with me in the warm spring air. Later, we crossed the street to the park, where we walked for a little while, then sat on a bench—they had brought along a cushion for my knobby back—watching the cyclists and in-line skaters speeding past. It was a grace-blessed day; the sun was warm, people were gay, and we were happy. For me, it was like an emergence from prison: I sat there almost like an ordinary person, with my children, in the sun, watching a world I was no longer disconnected from. After we returned, Rob walked to a nearby Mideast restaurant and brought back baba ganoush and hummus and tabouli and lentils and stuffed grape leaves and lamb and pita bread, and we ate together on the terrace. It was the first meal I had fully enjoyed since the previous September. And it was the best Mother's Day in my memory.

By mid-May, I felt I no longer needed the nurses. Without them, I might fall when I got up in the middle of the night, but they were too expensive to keep on simply for that one task. Knowing they were counting on the pay, I told them to stay for another week, but I felt wasteful. Ursula would sit alone in my apartment night after night while I went out with one friend or another, to dinner or to movies, and she'd glare at me when I returned.

I was longing for my Berkshire house, but I could not go there without help. Rob drove us all up for the weekend. It was my first visit to the house since the previous fall, and by mid-May, the gardens were aflame with rhododendron and azalea, lilac and late tulips. In the visualizations I did twice a day while I had cancer, I had always ended up picturing myself at the Berkshire house. I started elsewhere—a Greek island, a small boat in the Mediterranean along the coast of Italy, in Venice, or a luscious landscape in the middle of the Serengeti or Ngorongoro—or places I had not been to but imagined—Majorca, Rio, Tierra del Fuego—but no matter how I pushed my mind, my vision always homed in on this house, this porch, in the midst of this garden. Then, I had not been sure I would ever see them again. Now, here I was. I was moved with gratitude that I still had this in my life.

I made a plan. It felt daring, but more than anything else that spring, this plan made me feel human again. I knew I could not live in the country by myself. I was still too weak to cook meals, or even bathe myself, much less carry groceries. I could not drive my car, a sports car with a manual shift that was too hard for me to maneuver now; I had tried to drive and found myself uncontrollably canting to the left, out of my lane. Also, I was terrified in cars. Even when driven by Rob (whom I trusted), I felt vulnerable, as if every nearby car was about to crush my body, even if our car was coming to a halt. Still, I no longer needed round-the-clock nursing. I wanted to hire someone who could cook and care for me but who could also be trusted to drive my Porsche. Since this person would be with me for much of the day, I wanted it to be someone I liked—an equal, not a servant.

My friend Candace Hogan was a bit down on her

luck that summer. She had a somewhat boring job in the city, but I knew she loved to spend summers in the country, especially in the Berkshires. And I enjoy her greatly. After some negotiation, she agreed to do it, and when the nurses left, she began to stay in the guest room in my apartment. She helped me to shower, cooked dinners (she kept her day job), and on the weekend drove me to the country. Isabelle made my morning tea and poured me an Ensure for lunch.

However, a new problem suddenly arose on Thursday. I was having trouble swallowing, because of a narrowing in my throat. I knew that if I could not swallow my own saliva, I would die, and in terror called my oncologist. Unperturbed, he told me to call Dr. Gerdes at S-K and schedule an endoscopy. Luckily, it took only a telephone call to Dr. Gerdes's office to schedule the operation for the following Monday— the first of many such procedures I had over the next years.

An endoscopy involves sliding a thin wire down the esophagus to open up a channel for swallowing. The wire carries a tiny camera to photograph what is going on in the depth of the organ, so it is a diagnostic tool as well. With each operation, a vein had to be found for an IV. This was the hardest part of the process. The operation is painless: I was under anesthesia when they slipped the wire down my throat. Once, I woke up in the middle of the operation and told them I was awake: they immediately increased the anesthetic. I had felt only a pressure in my throat. Among the drugs they gave me was Demerol, which always cheers me up; I wake up laughing and joking. The kids say I should take it regularly. A few times, my throat was bruised by the wire or, perhaps, the camera.

The narrowing of the esophagus is caused by scar tissue as the ulcerations in the throat close up and heal. After my first operation, I asked Dr. Gerdes if the ulcerations would ever heal completely and the scar tissue disappear. This attentive man gives his patients thoughtful, honest answers; he said, regretfully, that he did not know. This surprised me: I still did not realize how rare was survival from esophageal cancer, or comprehend how terminal my diagnosis had been. Only later did I deduce that no patient treated at S-K for esophageal cancer had lived long enough for Dr. Gerdes to discover whether radiation-generated ulcerations healed. I gathered this mainly from his jubilation two years later when he announced that the ulcerations had indeed healed and explained that I was a miracle: he had held few hopes for my future.

Still, the problem with the esophagus became a source of anxiety when I was better and wanted to travel, because I could never predict how much time would elapse before an endoscopy would be necessary. When I needed one, I needed it right away: being unable to swallow triggers panic and can lead to death. If I wanted to plan a trip, I would have to consider when I might need another operation. Would it be in ten weeks or twenty? I never solved this problem: the six endoscopies I had were spaced twelve to thirty weeks apart. But this was one problem that ended. Blessedly.

May and June 1993 were filled with social events, doctors' appointments, and weekends in the Berkshires. I was not writing or reading seriously, and despite my editing of *Our Father,* I was not certain of my mental sharpness. I was a member of the Harvard Graduate School Council, which was meeting early in June, and I had decided to attend what would be my last meeting (the term of office is three years)—it would be my first trip since my illness had begun. Then Harvard wrote that they were giving me the Centennial Medal, an award for accomplishment. A few years before, I had attended the ceremony when they awarded it to Susan Sontag. So I *had* to go.

Candace flew up to Boston with me, the luggage and I in her charge. We stayed at a Cambridge hotel, and Candace accompanied me to the cocktail party and dinner the night preceding the meeting. I barely got through these events, cruelly aware of my fragility and fatigue. I cannot say I enjoyed them, as I had in the past; I was testing myself, and just barely passing. But the next day, at the ceremony and luncheon, I found that some of my best old Harvard pals had been gathered and brought to Cambridge. LeAnne Schreiber, Michael Malone, Maureen Quilligan, Janet and Tim Murray, were all seated at my table, and their familiar boisterous good humor (not normal at these events) got me through the praising speeches and past my own sense of frailty. I had a marvelous time and found myself unexpectedly moved by the event.

After arriving at Logan for the return trip, Candace and I discovered that all flights had been canceled. I did not trust trains in bad weather; I had a terrible memory of a snowy day when flights were canceled and my New York–Boston train took twelve hours. So we rented a big Lincoln Continental, which Candace drove to New York that night, the two of us light-hearted and giggly as we whizzed along the empty dark highways.

Candace drove us to the country again that week-end. I could not yet stay there permanently, because I had too many doctors' appointments. The following weekend, Rob drove me up. I had invited my father, my sister, and Fred for Father's Day; except for the fact that the children did all the cooking and cleaning up, it felt almost as if I were well.

At the end of June, I began to work again. I noted this fact on my calendar in large scrawled writing. The Shakespeare Festival in Stratford, Canada, had earlier that year asked me to speak there in August. That festival has mounted fascinating productions of Shakespeare over the years and is one of the few places where the directors credit my Shakespeare interpretations in the program notes. I was thrilled to be able to make up for my cancellation the year before—I felt I was resuming my life.

On June 25, Candace drove us to the country, where I planned to spend the summer. I started to write an essay on *King John,* one of the Stratford productions for that year. I had not worked since the October before, when, on my laptop in the hospital, I finished the final draft of *Our Father* and wrote the first two chapters of a satirical novel about an aging woman's ludicrous love affair. Now, using the laptop, I sat on my chaise on the screened porch and wrote for several hours a day. I was happy. I was not my old self—I was still weak and unable to do many things—but I could work, and I took huge pleasure in that, as I always have. Snags and problems may frustrate, but they also increase the pleasure of an intense effort. After I finished writing the Shakespeare talk, early in July, I began working on the copyedited version of *Our Father;* when that was finished, near the end of the month, I revised the Shakespeare speech and immediately began revising a long history of women I had worked on for twelve years, trying once more to cut it. It had been a five-thousand-page manuscript; it was now down to three thousand pages. I had to cut it further.

I also went swimming every warm day, and by July I was able to drive the car locally, to my physical therapist. Candace and I did errands together, and I supervised while she cooked—very well. The children came up most weekends, Candace's time off. It was a treat to see them so often.

Late in July, the coven came for a weekend. I had a catered dinner and a picnic lunch (salade niçoise) prepared for the next day, when we went to Tanglewood. The following weekend, the kids and I saw a play about Brecht at a local art gallery and took a picnic lunch to Tanglewood on Sunday. Some Saturday afternoons, we went to hear early music played by Aston Magna, a magnificent group that plays in a church in Great Barrington. A lovely summer, filled with pleasure, it was far better than I could have hoped if I had let myself hope. I was not recovered, but I was well enough to feel grateful I had survived. I was getting stronger week by week.

When the time came to go to Canada, I decided to see if I could do it on my own. Though Candace was supposed to have the weekends off, she was willing to accompany me. But I felt so good that I wanted to test myself. I would not have to do much walking, and if I could get someone to carry my bag, I should be able to do it. So I did. Candace drove me to New York (I still could not manage that journey), and a hired car took me to the airport. I arrived in Stratford on Friday, August 6; that night, I had dinner with Jean Davison, a Canadian librarian. I had met her in 1980, on a British-sponsored tour to China (the only way an American could visit China in those days). We took a train from Victoria Station to the English Channel, sailed across, then took trains to Paris, Berlin west and east, Warsaw (where Polish friends unexpectedly met me with over-flowing bouquets), Moscow, Ulan Bator (where we were stuck for ten days, owing to a flood in the Gobi Desert), then on to Beijing, Nanking, Shanghai, Nan-ch'ang, Ch'ang-sha, Canton, and Hong Kong. It was a tumultuous journey, partly because of a jejune tour guide and partly because the directors had no backup plan for disasters. But I became friendly with a few of the tourists and had since corresponded with Jean.

I was to speak on Sunday. On Saturday, Pat Quigley, my festival liaison, took me sightseeing in Stratford, which had barely changed since my last visit, over two decades earlier. The next day, I was blessed with a wonderful audience for my speech; it was made up mostly of women (as are all my audiences), but these were feminist Shakespeare scholars, and their questions were brilliant; they were a great pleasure. Afterward, I had lunch with Michele Landsberg, the *Toronto*

Star columnist, and her friend Ellen De Noon. We had so much fun together that I invited them to the Berkshires for a visit.

Some things were hard for me on this trip (for example, my bedroom was a flight of stairs up from the sitting room in my hotel, the bathroom on the floor below). I was a little slow; it was not easy for me to walk around the town. But my only serious problem arose from my vanity—I felt humiliated by the shakiness visible in my gait when I walked to the podium. In the end, I shrugged it off, telling myself it would disappear as I got stronger, that my difficulty was a result of muscle weakness from the coma.

Later in August, Gloria Beckerman and Perry Birnbaum, my old Hofstra friends, came to the Berkshire house for a couple of days. Candace made wonderful meals and was such a warm hostess that they both fell in love with her. The day they left, the kids appeared, and the next morning we took off for Maine.

This was Barbara and Rob's idea. They love the beauty of the state and often camp out among the pine trees and hike along the coast. This year, they invited Jamie and me along. They knew I could not camp out, and consulting us all along, they planned our ten days, making reservations at bed-and-breakfasts. We went first to Freeport, where Jamie and Barbara indulged their love of shopping while Rob sighed and I expostulated about the boring sameness of the merchandise. We stopped to see Esther and Bob Broner at Deer Isle, where they go every August; they were having a big party that day, which we briefly joined. I was thrilled to see the coastline from their house: Bob had given me a sketch of it when I was ill, and I sometimes used it to visualize the ideal spot. Indeed, it was that.

Then we drove to Bar Harbor and did the usual tourist things—the whale watch, the boat trip around the coast, visits to the fishing villages, Acadia National Park on Mount Desert Island, a drive over Mount Cadillac, and dinner at the Jordan Pond Restaurant, where three of us ate lobster. Rob has never gotten over the time I cooked lobster at home, when he was eight or so. I put the lobsters in salt water in the sink, to keep them alive until dinner, and one crawled out. Rob saw it moving across the kitchen floor and understood that it was to be cooked alive. He has never eaten lobster since, and every time *we* did, he would cry out in a tiny falsetto, "I want to live! I want to live!"

From Bar Harbor we went to Moosehead Lake, which Jamie found barbaric. It was cold there, and our cabin was a bit primitive but faced the gorgeous lake. Jamie and Barbara had fun in a pedal boat, we took a trip on a small motorboat to study wildlife and on a large one to survey the extent of the lake. We ate one night at the Road Kill Café, whose menu inspired us for the next few days to compete in inventing disgusting names for roadkill dishes. Our competition, totally juvenile, amused us greatly.

During our return, we stayed overnight at a bed-and-breakfast in Portsmouth, New Hampshire, a town that enchanted us. It had an old section, dating back only to the turn of the century but charming nevertheless; Strawberry Banke was a wonderful museum of houses from the original settlement saved from demolition, restored or made into architectural displays. Some of them are old dwellings and shops, some are almost mansions. In one two-family house, the house on the right was restored to its condition in the eighteenth century, as a shop and dwelling; the house on the left, equally old, had last been inhabited in the 1930s and was left with furniture and household items of that time. The general store also dated to the 1930s. These two buildings seized me, carried me almost into tears. I am rooted in the 1930s, and its artifacts carried me back to a childhood that, unhappy as it was, tugged at me.

Our idyll ended, alas: I had been transported—literally and figuratively—by the trip and hated to come home. But within a few days, I had guests: Michele and Ellen from Toronto. It was September now, no swimming, but the days were still soft and golden. When my guests left, I got to work reading page proofs for *Our Father;* then I returned to the history book. Over the weekend, my sweet nephew Ricky Smith and his wife, Julia, came up to take me out to dinner at a local restaurant, and we had a bubbly evening.

It was time to go back to New York. Candace drove me down, and we parted: she went back to her old life, and I was going to try to take care of myself. Of course, I still had Isabelle to do marketing and errands, but the rest I would have to undertake. Over the summer, I had progressed to the point where I could nervously take a shower alone (but not a bath), could lift items that were not heavy (not, for instance, a pot of cooked pasta), and could drive for half an hour—not more. I could work at my computer if I piled pillows behind me and leaned back as I worked.

I cannot say I ever felt triumphant—I was too damaged for that—but there was a satisfaction in being able to get in a cab by myself and attend a PEN board meeting, the first in almost a year; and to get to Gloria's house the next night, for a coven meeting, and be able to swallow, to *eat*.

Wanting to make amends for my teary blame of them at our previous formal meeting, I wrote a poem for the event. To compliment them, I drew on Rimbaud's *Une Saison en Enfer,* a title that I felt described my experience as well. Rimbaud, in an experiment, had set out to "derange" all his senses, wishing to become a *voyant,* a seer, to transcend ordinary life, to arrive at the "Unknown." He believes that the Poet/*voyant* can realize an ideal "harmonious Life" such as existed in ancient times. The poet will then liberate men, animals, language, and even women, whose "endless servitude will be overthrown." (Rimbaud dedicated *Une Saison en Enfer* to his mother: "my first teacher of poetry / in literature and in life.") Using alcohol, hashish, and other intoxicants, he writes as a "soul condemned to hell," in delirium, in torment, hallucinating. In the poem, the poet is also condemned to aloneness, sometimes perceiving himself as a great artist in process of transcending life, and at other times seeing himself as a mere peasant. Throughout the poem, love is banished as inadequate to the poet's need.

I wanted to compare my experience with his, and incidentally, a female with a male approach. My ingestion of poisons was not by choice but by necessity, and I sought, not revelation, but recovery. I, too, discovered hell, but along the way *I* discovered a harmonious life—my own. The difference was that I was so surrounded with love that, resistant to love as I am, I *felt* loved for the first time in my life. My friends and my children had renewed my life by transforming hell into a kind of heaven.

In my poem, I spoke of this and of my gratitude to be alive despite everything; I told my friends that they and my children had made me feel more loved than I had ever felt as a child.

During that week of September—the first week in which I could move on my own since the Christmas before, the first time since the previous October that I was strong enough to walk around the city by myself, and sit through a movie and eat popcorn, and go home and write an article—my spirits flew. I *was* going to get better, I was already much better, I was going to get my old life back and be my old self again. I *would.*

I was elated the day after the coven meeting, when Jamie drove us up to the Berkshire house for the weekend. Eager to see Innisfree, a "cup garden" in Millbrook, New York, we went on Sunday. It is composed of only natural features of the landscape, somewhat manipulated, and surrounds a lake; a path leads from one almost contained environment to another—thus, a cup garden, based on Japanese models. I made an error and forgot to take drinking water; nor did I realize at the outset that once on the path, one could only turn back or finish the walk. There were no shortcuts, and the walk was way over a mile long, perhaps two miles—a bit of a strain for me. This was not a problem until we were about two-thirds along. I was tired, but there was no respite. I had to finish. I did. And a kind woman at the end shared her bottled water with me. I was tired, but no harm done, I thought.

The next day, my back ached. Luckily, I had an appointment for a laying on of hands by my physical therapist that day. Myofascial therapy eased the pain slightly, but by the time Jamie and I got back to New York, I was in severe pain. I called a masseuse who had been recommended to me, explained how much pain I was in, and she came over and gave me a treatment that eased it somewhat. Then, at the very end, she said, "I'm going to give you a little shiatsu." Before I could protest, she banged down on my back. I screamed.

She had broken my back.

FALL 1993—SPRING 1994

The masseuse was so frightened by my terrible scream that she would not leave until a doctor examined me. I called Edie Langner, my internist, whom I had not seen for a year, and she persuaded her then partner, Lucy Painter, to come to my apartment. But back problems are invisible. By the time Dr. Painter arrived, I was merely in pain. She believed I was in spasm and told me to rest for a few days.

The next day, the pain was unendurable; in my experience, the pain does not become severe until the day after a break. All my friends agreed that back pain was "the worst." I could not move without weeping—getting out of or into bed was truly awful—but I assumed this was what back spasms felt like. I remained in bed for three days; on the fourth day, I pulled myself out. I went downstairs, piled my desk chair with pillows, and returned to work.

Reviewing my calendar for this period, I am startled to see how I drove myself despite my broken back. I sat at my computer, revising the history book. That I lost only three days of work seems inconceivable to me now, remembering the agony I was in. My calendar claims I went to the theater, took my father to an ophthalmologist, made dinner for him, accompanied him to the hospital for a cataract operation, made dinner a second night because he had to see the doctor again the next morning, having developed a minor problem in surgery. I remember doing these things. I do not remember how I felt. I also saw real estate agents, because I planned to sell my apartment.

My call to Dr. Langner aroused her concern, and she called and asked to see me. I went in on October 12, almost two weeks after my back was broken, and told her how much pain I was in. Edie asked for details about my illness: I had not seen her since the cancer was first diagnosed. There was no easy way to do so; I was being treated elsewhere and had no reason to consult her. It never occurred to me to keep her aware of my situation, for her to oversee it. The specialists would not defer to her, I knew. And I did not want to present myself to her during my cancer treatments: her husband—who was treated at least partly at Sloan-Kettering—had died shortly before my diagnosis, and I did not want to be a reminder. I knew she was heartbroken.

But now I laid my problems out before her with huge relief. Eager to know all the details, she never once made me feel rushed, never once acted inattentive. This was the answer! She *wanted* to oversee my whole self, medically, something I had longed for. She sent me to a back specialist, who told me to wear a brace and prescribed Dilaudid. The pain pills helped if I took them continually, but that I did only for a while.

Meantime, my throat had closed up again, and I made an appointment for another endoscopy. I knew, though, that there was someone looking out for me, someone I could call without embarrassment or anxiety that my call would not be returned, as sometimes happened with my oncologist.

Over the weekend, I went to the movies and lunch with Herb Weiss and had lunch the next day with Carol and Esther. Monday morning, I entered S-K for the operation. Rob accompanied me; then we went back to my house and ordered dinner (probably from Rainbow Chicken). Charlotte had invited me to visit the following weekend, and since her country house was closer than mine, I thought I could manage the drive. But I was only about three-quarters of the way when I doubled over with pain. I don't know how I made it; I drove in a twisted position, then lay in agony on Charlotte's couch for the rest of the weekend. Charlotte and her friend Miranda took me home, one of them driving my car, the other, her own.

Edie Langner had suggested physiotherapy for my back and sent me to a dance therapist in the Ansonia building. When I saw her Monday morning, she gave me a treatment and told me to obtain a back brace. I finally bought one, wearing it that evening to the Met. Earlier that season, I had ordered various opera tickets, trying to make up for the wonders I had missed during the past two years. Two productions were scheduled for that week—*Stiffelio* at the Met and *Madama Butterfly* (the original version, which I had never seen) at the City Opera.

The next day, I went to my oncologist. He took my back pain seriously, because after being eliminated elsewhere, cancers frequently invade the bones, especially the spine. I had a bone scan that afternoon. When he called to tell me the results, he said, "I'm sorry to tell you . . . ," and my heart stopped. But he continued, ". . . that you do have a compression fracture." He had sandbagged me again. So it was not until the end of October that I finally realized my back had broken, that the pain was not from spasm, and that there had been good reason for me to weep. He told me that the radiation had probably harmed my spine (although of course I had not had enough to make this happen). It was sawdust; I had severe osteoporosis and could have another compression fracture easily. I had to be careful.

Wearing the brace, and down to two pain pills a day—in the morning and at night—I had dinner with my publisher, Jim, attended a reading of a brilliant new play by Janet Neipris, and went to the movies and dinner with Gloria. But my next session of physiotherapy put me into agony again. I stopped treatments. But I continued my social life. The calendar for the following weeks reads as if I gritted my teeth, determined to have my old life back no matter what: there were parties or dinners almost every night, an evening at a cabaret starring Donna McKechnie, and a long afternoon spent participating in a conversation about pornography and censorship that would be printed in *Ms.* magazine. During the day, I worked on the history book revision, had back X rays and an MRI, met real estate agents.

By November, the pain had moderated a bit, but it was always present, its dull ache reminding me not to move too quickly or in certain ways. I wore the brace every day, although I questioned whether it helped. I now took the Dilaudid only once a day. I could not stand up straight long enough to prepare a meal, so I hired some young men to come and cook for me on the evenings when I was home. Charlotte recommended an osteopath with a tremendous reputation and self-esteem to match. But his superexpensive treatments did not help at all.

On November 20, my dear friend Beatrix Campbell traveled from England to spend my birthday with me. Unable to come while I was sick, she made a surprise visit now. We talked for hours, our conversations always among the most brilliant and lively of any I have. Our subject is usually politics, her specialty, but we go far afield. The kids had arranged a dinner party at the Café des Artistes, one of my favorite restaurants (it serves pot-au-feu, a rarity in America). Then I dragged Bea shopping: I had to get birthday gifts for Rob and Jamie. If she did not enjoy that, she made the best of it. Bea and I went to the Met to hear *Russalka,* and one of the cooks prepared a lovely dinner at my house for Bea, Ann Jones, and me.

Bea was soon gone, but my social calendar was filled in to the end of the year. I had tickets for *Les Troyens, Angels in America,* and *All in the Timing;* there were parties at Lisa Alther's and at Alix Kates Shulman's, a coven meeting, a Christmas Eve party, a dinner with Gloria and Carol. But first was a dinner with Charlotte, at an old French restaurant on the West Side. We had finished eating, when I almost doubled over with a pain in my side. Perhaps it was gas—had I let myself go too long without eating? That always caused problems for me. Perhaps it was the brace, which was extremely tight, confining my lower back and waist. I told Charlotte I had to go home. On arriving, I removed the brace, but the pain persisted. I put myself to bed and lay there, feeling awful. During the night, I began to shiver; my teeth chattered, and I could not get warm.

This continued into the morning, when it occurred to me I might have a fever and that it might be wise to call Edie—I might be coming down with flu. When Edie heard my symptoms, her voice rose; she told me to get to the emergency room at St. Luke's–Roosevelt *immediately,* that she and Lucy would meet me there, that I had an infection, probably in my kidney. Worried about my reaction to the hospital's emergency room, she told me not to be upset by it; she and Lucy would meet me there and walk me through.

Dazed, I dressed and tried to pack for the hospital, but I was befuddled. Isabelle helped me. I called the kids and told them what was happening, and they said they would meet me as soon as they could. By the time I reached the ER, I was pretty sick: I have little memory of what occurred. I know the children were there; I don't recall seeing Edie or Lucy until much later, long after I was admitted. A new doctor, a urologist recommended by Edie, Frank Lowe, examined me and said I had a kidney infection and needed what sounded to me like an operation. No operation, I said. I would not be invaded.

But I was in no condition to be making such a judgment. I was in and out of delirium, in terrible pain, my whole body shaking. The next day, or perhaps it was two days later, Frank and Edie approached me together, almost formally. They told me I would die if I did not have the procedure they recommended. It was not actually an operation, they said, but the insertion of a tube that would allow the pus to drain from my kidney, which was impeded because I had so many kidney stones. Believing I was on the verge of death, I agreed.

They rushed me into the operating room. I was given anesthesia and remember little about it except that as they were wheeling me out, Dr. Lowe turned to the doctor who had assisted him and said, "We got her just in time. Another hour and she was dead." The second doctor concurred.

Six months later, I was a patient in the same operating room (I would be in that room often over the next years) and met one of the nurses who assisted the first time. She cried out when she saw me. Embracing me, she said she was so happy to see me, so happy I was better. She remembered me very well: "It was just before Christmas, and I had a plane reservation—I was going home for the holidays—but Dr. Lowe said I had to stay, that you were dying and needed this procedure, so I stayed, and oh, God, you were so sick, I'll never forget it. He said afterward that we'd saved your life. I felt so proud." Then she kissed me.

Sociobiologists who emphasize the aggressive self-ishness of the human species never consider our ten-dency to love those for whom we make a sacrifice and the place of that love in our lives. Although I recall that nurse with affection, I don't even know her name. I'm sure I asked it when she spoke to me, but I did not manage to retain it. She will never forget me, though, not because of anything I am or did, but because of what *she* did. What she did helped to save my life; she enriched me. But her sacrifice most of all enriched *her;* my surviving enriched her; her love for me enriched her. All this love she offers—for surely I am not the only patient to benefit from it—will probably carry her into a contented old age. I believe that is the way life works. Instead of looking for a gene for altruism, students of human behavior should consider how altru-istic behavior benefits the actor, how love enriches the lover more than the beloved, how virtue truly is its own reward and aggressive behavior its own punish-ment.

The tube was inserted, but I remained quite sick. The infection drained slowly, for the kidney stones continued to impede it, and my fever remained high. I had the usual visitors in the hospital, but was not my usual cheerful "hospital" self. I felt aggrieved, felt that things were stacked against me. Edie and I had worked so hard to keep me well: Edie, always worried about my damaged kidneys, had checked my urine regularly for signs of a kidney infection. She had done it only *one week* before I got sick. And I scrupulously followed her instructions. What more could we do? I had just recov-ered from the worst of the back pain, just begun to heal. I had tried so hard to function despite it, to keep a positive attitude, to recover my old life and well-being. And here I was spending another Christmas in the hospital, all the planned holiday events forgone.

I was as low as I had been since I woke from the coma. I was sick of being sick, sick of being in hospitals, having my body invaded and stuck and drained and listened to by stranger after stranger. I can't count the doctors who treated me or whom I consulted through my illness, because I did not see some of them, did not know many of them, and do not remember all of them. But I saw, knew, and remember about fifty different doctors. I felt like Beckett's creature crawling through mud in *How It Is,* who continually deludes himself that he/she sees light ahead, that he/she is getting someplace. But I was even worse: I kept encountering horrors in the mud and kept trying to get past or ignore them. I did not know how much longer I could fight. I did not want to live a self-pitying life, but I was overcome with despair.

The infection was so stubborn that the doctors did not want to release me without an extra measure of protection, and urged me to have a stent inserted in my kidney. A thin plastic tube that I would not feel or see, the stent would permit drainage in the organ despite the kidney stones. I saw these during a sonogram, and they were certainly plentiful. (I do not know if I had them before I became ill; chemotherapy can cause kidney stones.) I asked the urologist if it was not possible to get rid of kidney stones; he said it was but that there were two sorts of stones, each requiring different treatment; he gave me some vague reason why that could not be done now. So I agreed to the stent, which the urologist promised would protect me against further infections. It was during the procedure to insert the stent that I met again the nurse who had earlier given up her plane ticket to save my life.

After a two-week stay in the hospital, I was very weak. A couple of years later, a nephrologist told me that for unknown reasons, hospitalization was particularly hard on kidney patients, who require a week to recover from each day in the hospital. It would take fourteen weeks, over three months, to recover from two weeks of hospitalization. But I did not know this then, and felt low and hopeless and grouchy as I stumbled around my apartment, once again weak and not in control of my movements.

Our Father was published in early January, and I had been scheduled to make a publicity tour. The tour was canceled because of my hospitalization, and nothing else was done—no ads, no promotion. This harmed sales of the book. And given that I had gone without working for almost two years and had over half a million dollars' worth of medical bills (not all covered by insurance), I needed the book to do well. Beyond that, the reviews upset me. They described the book as a "good read," a "page turner." But I had planted myself deeply in this book; it was on one level a response to the most important book I had ever read (Dostoevsky's *The Brothers Karamazov*). But then, reviewers, female or male, rarely treat fiction by women seriously; with a few exceptions, who, it is decided early on, are "serious," women are reviewed as if they write with their uteruses. Women's fiction is assumed to be auto-biographical, based on the writer's sexual and emotional life. Although incest is important in *Our Father*, its major theme is not incest, as everyone wrote, but four sisters' hatred for one another, based partly in their profound disagreement about the nature of life. Not only did no reviewer ask how incest fits within this larger theme of female disharmony, but none even noticed the theme.

Writing is a lonely occupation to begin with, but the sense of aloneness is hugely compounded when a book receives absolutely no comprehension. The cause of this obtuseness is sometimes stupidity but most often is blindness caused by the sex of the writer. That most women's writing is not serious is a prejudice shared by female and male reviewers; they approach the work of the two sexes with different expectations. I knew that after such a dumb response, I was not easily again going to be able to muster the passion and intellectual fervor with which I wrote *Our Father*.

Two weeks after my release from St. Luke's–Roosevelt, I had to enter Sloan-Kettering for another endoscopy. Although this was not a painful procedure and Dr. Gerdes was always pleasant, it was nevertheless another day in the hospital, a day of waiting, undressing once more in a cold metal locker room, getting into chilly paper hospital garb, waiting, waiting, waiting, having needles stuck in my arm, lying on a cold metal table in an operating room, being asked to sign a form stating that I have been told that I could possibly be damaged or killed by the procedure about to take place, then recovering slowly in a huge warehouse of a room. It was another day in the elephant dung. I was deathly tired of it.

I seemed to need much medical attention in the weeks after my release, and between the many doctors' appointments and my depression, I saw few friends. My sister helped me out of this. She knew I normally spent the winter in Florida, and understanding that I was not yet physically able to take care of myself, she offered to go with me, to help me manage. Hating the cold, I happily accepted, and at the end of January we flew down together.

Florida was hard for me. The building I live in is relatively new, and its doors, all up to modern codes, are so heavy I can barely open them. When the wind was high (as it almost always is, winters) the doors to outside were impossible for me. Even now, I can open the door to my apartment only by leaning my entire weight against it and slowly pushing forward. My sister's help was invaluable. She drove the car I rented; she opened the damned doors. She carried bags of heavy vegetables from the market, and the half-bushels of the Honeybell oranges I love. Together we prepared meals and cleaned up.

It was my first post-cancer experience of trying to manage virtually on my own, and I found it very hard. Not being able to do things, or trying and failing, made me irritable when I was in pain or when things went wrong. I did not like this and, looking for excuses, told myself it was caused by my constant pain. I did not know that the irritability was a symptom of trauma.

Still, Isabel and I had fun together, and as I grew stronger, I once more became convinced that I would fully recover. And, too, my depression passed. The year before, I had agreed to extravagant plans for the spring, believing despite my weakness that I could realize them. I had agreed to go to Holland to promote *Our Father;* to attend the Adelaide Book Fair in Australia; and, a bit later, to go to England for a week of promotion. Bad weather in the Northeast stymied Isabel's and my return from Florida, but we finally got back to New York. A few days later, I was on a plane to Amsterdam.

It was horribly cold there, and the streets were icy; with my weak body, broken back, and sawdust spine, I did not dare to walk around the city. Still, I was overjoyed to be in Amsterdam again, recalling my melancholy intimations of mortality on my last visit. I had dinner with Annaville and Nettie, and with my lovable Dutch publisher, Maarten Asscher. But mostly I sat in the wonderful Hotel de l'Europe, being interviewed.

I returned to New York on a Friday night, did some telephone and television interviews with Australian media people (some of whom had interviewed me before I left for Holland), and on Monday evening flew to L.A. I stayed there for a night, and the next day took a cab up the coast to visit the Getty Museum. That this gorgeous building with its wonderful art could be created purely by money, not time, I found amazing. That night, I flew to Australia.

I had not been there in fifteen years and was expecting to encounter the same culture I saw in 1977 and 1979. At that time, Australians were xenophobic in the extreme, especially about blacks and Asians. Australian men were the current ugly Americans of the South Pacific; and many of the women journalists who interviewed me ended up weeping in my hotel room, an experience I never had elsewhere. In a fine restaurant in Melbourne, dining with a party of publishers, I listened in shock as a waiter told the table a long-drawn-out anti-Semitic joke.

But I had never been to Adelaide, a southern province famed for its art festival, held every two years. Getting to Adelaide took some time, and I was tired when I arrived, but I was whisked away by Mary Beasley, then CEO of the Department of Industrial Affairs of South Australia and chair of the suffrage centenary (South Australians were the first women in the world to win the vote, in 1894), and Susie Mitchell, chair of Adelaide Writers' Week in the Adelaide Festival of the Arts. They had the imaginative and humane idea of protecting the authors from the media for a weekend, to give them a chance to get to know each other, to recover from the long journey, and to see a little of Adelaide. This is not done at other festivals I have attended, and I found it a wonderful tonic. Instead of interviews, we were offered tours of the area's natural features, swims, and great boozy dinners. This weekend gave me a chance to get to know Deirdre Bair, whose fascinating, intelligent, and unswerving biography of Simone de Beauvoir had had the unfortunate effect of making me dislike intensely the woman who was my mentor; Sara Paretsky, whose mysteries I enjoy for their strong social conscience; and Rosie Scott, an Australian novelist whose work had impressed me with its breadth and humanity.

Back in the city, I was amazed at the Australia I saw. There were Asians everywhere, and the restaurants (which on my last visit had been much like provincial British restaurants serving food that hovered on the edge of inedibility) now offered an inventive indigenous cuisine influenced by Asian cooking—what in New York is called "Asian fusion." Everywhere the food was wonderful, and everywhere I saw signs of respect for or at least tolerance of aboriginal culture, Asian culture, and varied sexual adaptations.

The place was utterly different from the Australia of 1979. It is rare that a culture moves from narrow meanness to openness and harmony; the reverse is far more common. I was moved and impressed by the courage and decency of the white people of this continent, who had somehow dared to overcome their terror at being distant from their English and Irish roots, their fear of engulfment by peoples so apparently different, and their prejudices, enough to embrace at least the idea of openness and tolerance. The consequence, for those who have done so, is harmony and happiness: the Australia of 1994 was immeasurably happier than that of 1979.

With Rosie Scott, I wandered through the back streets of Adelaide and took a boat ride down its river. Her work is sensuously alive like that of few other writers—I can think only of Colette and Edna O'Brien—but also highly political. Reviewers tend not to see women's politics; those of us who address sexual politics are consigned to the "feminist" ghetto, and male reviewers discount female writers, like the Argentinian Luisa Valenzuela, who concern themselves with national or global problems. Rosie turned out to be as delectable a person as she is a writer, and although we got together only a few times, we still correspond fondly. Elmore Leonard was at the conference, but distant; as was a group of English novelists including David Lodge, whom I had met in the seventies—at a Joyce conference, I think. He looked so young then, I thought he was a student, when in fact he was already an accomplished novelist and teacher.

Susie and Mary took over my social life, escorting me to many festival events—a brilliant Mark Morris performance of Purcell's *Dido and Aeneas,* and a play by Patrick White, Australia's Nobelist. Judging by the play, which I walked out of, White had a cramped, narrow, mean mind, to which no bias was foreign. He represented the Australia I had encountered in the seventies. There were dinners with publishers and with Mary and Susie and Deirdre and Rosie in one or another of Adelaide's good restaurants, and of course interviews and panels and speeches. I flew from Adelaide to Sydney for more interviews and visited Peter Solomon, who had been a colleague of mine on the Harvard Graduate Council, and his wife and children. The highlight of my Sydney stay was what is called the Mardi Gras parade, although Mardi Gras had already passed. This huge parade, lasting hours, may be the highlight of the Sydney social season. Fortunately, friends of a friend, who met me in the city and generously took me about, had reserved a spot for us in a glass-walled room overlooking the parade route. Since I could not have stood for so many hours, I was grateful.

What was most astonishing, though, to a person who recalled the old Australia was that this is a gay parade. It opened with a group calling themselves Dykes on Bikes, young women in black who roared through triumphantly on their motorcycles, waving to the crowd, which cheered loudly. The overwhelming majority of the marchers were men, though, most in high blond beehive hairdos, six-inch heels, and sequined skintight dresses. How they could march for hours in that gear, I have no idea. Some mimed famous women—the favorites were Mary Tyler Moore, Doris Day, Jackie Kennedy, Margaret Thatcher, and Bronwyn Bishop, a shadow minister in the Liberal party, whose sin seems to have been being ambitious and female and having a blond beehive hairdo. Each time she appeared—and there were tens of her—a great roar went up from the crowd. My Australian friends tell me there was talk of Bishop becoming the next Prime Minister if the Liberals won the election, and that to avert this possibility, the press had been setting her up, preparing to cut her down. They succeeded. She is at present merely a deputy minister of the armed forces in the Liberal cabinet.

In the end, I found the parade a little upsetting, really insulting to women, as if protruding cone-shaped breasts, huge asses, exaggerated hairdos, high heels, and clinging dresses constituted the essence of woman-hood, which these men were claiming for their own. But in fact, these guys worship the penis, and where were the penises? There was only one that I saw, a missile mounted by a dozen men, ready to shoot off into space; the rest of the parade was devoted to exaggerated female sexual characteristics.

I do not believe in essential differences between the sexes and am happy when males claim the qualities usually ascribed to women—qualities like compassion, nurturance, cooperation, and tolerance. I think a greater emphasis on these attitudes is the only thing that can save the world. But it was not these qualities that were being celebrated. They celebrated the qualities possessed by a character in *Woman on the Edge of Time*, perhaps Marge Piercy's greatest book, whose hourglass-shaped body was created for male desire. The men in this parade were her clones.

On March 7, I left Sydney for Melbourne, to do promotion; then on March 9, I flew to the Great Barrier Reef. I have never been in a more idyllic spot. On Hayman Island, I stayed in a cottage right on the beach. The water was warm, and calm enough that weak as I was, with my damaged body, I could swim in it. I sat, reading, on a comfortable chaise, gazing out at the sea. I took a helicopter/boat trip to the reef itself, a rich, brilliant environment of colorful fish and underwater plants that extends for miles in the middle of the ocean. My brief visit fulfilled a longtime wish.

I truly enjoyed my stay in Australia, partly because I was feeling good there—stronger and more able than I'd felt since my first spinal fracture, and maybe stronger than at any time since I'd fallen ill. I began to weave illusions again, to imagine that I would be able to recover fully, be my "old self." It took forever to get home again—the day I had gained going to Australia was lost on the return trip. I arrived at JFK on Sunday, March 13, and was in Florida on the fifteenth. Rob and Barbara joined me there; they were to help me buy a new car. Much as I loved my Porsche, I had to find a car that held my back comfortably and was easy to drive, not requiring the many arm motions of a sports car. We went about this task efficiently, and in a few days I had bought a Lexus, which I drive to this day with great satisfaction. Rob and Barbara flew back home, and I settled in to live by myself for the first time since I'd been sick.

Living alone was still difficult, if not as hard as the year before, but I soon developed a new problem—frequent painful urination, often with blood. Though I had had this problem earlier, it suddenly became much more severe. I decided to find medical help locally. I had visited an internist when I first came to Florida, in the seventies. He knew my reputation, and my first published novel, and made some fuss over me. But his attitude during a gynecological exam he insisted on doing was such that I never went back to him. Since then, I had depended on my New York doctors—which was okay during the years when I had no medical problems. I investigated urologists and finally got a name from someone I trusted, but Edie had not heard of the man and, wary, suggested I return to New York and Dr. Lowe.

I decided to go to New York for the urological consultation in March, when my friends were celebrating. Esther was holding her Women's Seder (about which she wrote a book, *The Telling*) on March 26, and there was a birthday party for Gloria (two days late) the next day. I spent the rest of my time in New York in doctors' offices, but no one seemed to know what was wrong with me.

I had to go to England to do promotion for *Our Father,* and before I flew there, I needed another endoscopy. By April 11, when I left Florida for the season, I felt wonderful. Swimming every day had toned me up, strengthened me a bit, and I carried my hand luggage off the plane. It was a little heavy, perhaps twenty-odd pounds, but it seemed bearable for a while. And when it did not, did I stop, put it down, and look around for a skycap? I did not. I went on with it. The next day, in severe pain, I cursed myself, but it did not occur to me that I had again broken my back. I called in a masseur and packed for London.

I went through the rounds of interviews, lunches, dinners, and the theater, enjoying myself through my agony. I had my pain pills, but I think I never took enough for them to work. Edie tells me that when you are taking painkillers, you should *never* allow pain to creep in—that is, you should take a second pill before the first has completely worn off. I have never done that. It is a strange fact about pain, though, that you don't necessarily remember it later. I recall this London visit with pleasure.

At the end, I met up with Beatrix Campbell, and together we drove to Essex to visit Germaine Greer. She was as warm and full of sparkle and wit as ever. She went out to the garden of her beautiful old house and cut herbs and made us a delicious pasta dish with tomatoes and herbs for lunch. That night, she took us to dinner at Newnham, the Cambridge college where she teaches.

I wished that evening that Virginia Woolf were still alive to learn that Oxbridge women no longer had to endure terrible food. The dons at Newnham College ate exquisite *poussin*. We had great fun with these women, who are smart and savvy and sophisticated and amiable and friendly—utterly unlike the men at High Table at Oxford I have encountered.

The next day, we set off for Kent, a part of England I had only dipped into earlier. I wanted to see Canterbury Cathedral—which I found disappointing. It was the first church I'd seen in England that was marred by tawdry tourist surroundings—something more common abroad, in places like Mont-Saint-Michel and Saint Peter's. Bea and I stayed in a strange inn that seemed to be furnished with fun-house remainders but which served elaborate meals. We drove through the beautiful Kent countryside, and again I silently blessed the fates that allowed me to make such a trip despite my physical state.

MAY 1994–DECEMBER 1996

U pon returning, I had to move almost immediately from the apartment where I'd lived for fifteen years, which I had sold. Moving, with my aching back, was an ordeal and not as efficiently managed as earlier moves. An additional complication was that my dear assistant, Isabelle de Cordier, had just left me, having after many years of searching found a job in her specialty, architecture. She came after work, though, as usual doing as much as she could to help me.

My Central Park West apartment had always been too large for me—eight rooms and five bathrooms for one person seemed to me a little obscene right from the beginning, but I could not resist its gorgeous view of the park. Worried about buying it, superstitious, I suppose, I had asked my mother's advice. It's so big, I said; suppose the day comes when I can't afford to keep it up. Will I be brokenhearted? No, she said. You'll be glad to see the end of it. "We fall in love with places, but then we get tired of them," she said. "There will come a time when you'll want to leave it." She was right: the only things I would ever miss were my wonderful dressing room–bathroom and the stall shower, from inside which you could see the park reflected in the bathroom mirror; the working fireplace in my study; the large kitchen; and the doormen, who were so sweet and warm, they always made me feel welcomed home. The problem was finding places to put furnishings, paintings, and, above all, books from a large apartment. I regretted only breaking up my library, but after giving about a third of the books to a Berkshire library, I discovered my own collection was actually rejuvenated.

That spring, I gave readings at Crone's bookstore in Boston and at Harbourfront in Toronto. On my return, I saw my oncologist, who ordered an MRI; it showed that my back had indeed broken for the second time the previous April. But again there was no cancer. By now, of course, the fracture was less painful, but my range of motion was becoming more and more limited. Edie found a wonderful new therapist for me, Frania Zins, a Feldenkrais practitioner, who over years of treatments has helped me to grow stronger, stand straighter, and move so as not to exacerbate pain. Although I still feel almost constant pain, it is far milder than it was, despite a third compression fracture, which occurred in January 1996.

For the most part that spring, I relaxed in the beauty of the Berkshire countryside. The coven came up for a weekend. But the day they arrived, I began to bleed rather copiously, which frightened me. After much difficulty—it was the Fourth of July weekend—I reached both a doctor (albeit a stranger to me) *and* an available pharmacist; Gloria and Carol went to pick up a prescription. I also called Harold Greenberg, Barbara's husband, who calmed my anxiety—seeing a lot of blood is terrifying, when there seems to be no reason for it. I would have to go to New York for treatment, but still unable to drive myself that far, I put it off.

The following weekend, I had a large family party (the kids did most of the cooking and cleanup), after which my sister and Fred Baron drove me back to New York. A CT scan next day confirmed that there was no cancer in kidney or bladder. (Once you have had cancer, it is the first thing doctors check for.) The day after, my urologist removed the stent, for it was that which was causing the bleeding. He wanted to insert a fresh one, but I demurred. The stent was as much trouble as the kidney, I thought: I would take my chances without one. This was a bad decision.

Charlotte drove me back up to the Berkshires, where I planned to spend the rest of the summer. Having finished revising the history book, I could start a new work, and I picked up the novel I had begun in the hospital during the last months of chemotherapy. I started this novel, called *My Summer with George,* with the idea that I would try to write something light for a change. At the time, my life was full of blank dread, and I wanted to be—I wondered if I *could* be—comical, satirical. To write the novel I had in mind would require entirely different talents from *Our Father:*

not intensity but a light touch; not intellectual argument but mocking glances at serious ideas; not profound emotional conflict but absurd emotions couched in everyday language. Not only was I not sure I could do it; I was not sure I wanted to. But I persisted.

I had guests all week from August 8 to August 14. The last set was Linsey Abrams and Ann Volks, who came for a weekend, at the end of which I was stricken. I prepared meals but could not eat them, and I was doubled over in pain. But the pain was not like the last kidney infection, and I did not know what to make of it. The day after they left, I felt so sick that I had to call an ambulance and ask to be taken to the local hospital, Fairview. This charming place, with a mere fourteen rooms, has an excellent if limited staff, with few specialists. They fed me antibiotics, diagnosed a kidney infection, and told me I was fortunate, because the visiting urologist would be there the next day. Arriving, he insisted that I have myself moved up to Pittsfield, where he could insert a tube into my kidney that would empty into a bag outside my body. This would have the great benefit, he added enthusiastically, of allowing him to inject iodine (which he could not do internally, since it might kill me—although he didn't tell me that, I knew it), thus allowing them to see what was going on inside me. Hearing this, I called the (excellent) local internist and demanded to be taken to New York.

Arranging the ride to the city took forever. The internist wanted to be sure that I would be safe during the long trip, so he wanted medical personnel aboard the ambulance with me. Their presence raised the price charged by the local ambulance service for this jaunt to over $1,500. The trip was indeed long and very uncomfortable—for all the doctor's concern, I would have been less miserable in the back seat of, say, a Lincoln Town Car. When I asked the pleasant young paramedic accompanying me for a Tylenol—I was feeling feverish—he told me he did not have even an aspirin. By the time I reached St. Luke's–Roosevelt, my temperature was 105 degrees.

I spent nine days in the hospital, developing pneumonia while I was there. I also had a pain in my arm and chest; when I told the nurse I might have had a heart attack, she ignored me. I allowed the urologist to reinsert a new stent; clearly I could not manage without one. Immediately on my release, Rob and Barbara drove me back to the Berkshires for what remained of the summer. Weak, downhearted, weary of the whole situation, I tried once more to frame my mind toward acceptance and serenity. Edie advised me to find a doctor in the Berkshires, in case of emergencies. The fine internist who had cared for me at Fairview was not accepting new patients, and I was sent to his young associate, who lectured me for over an hour but did not recall who I was when I called him in need the next day.

That need occurred over Labor Day weekend. The kids were visiting and we had planned some pleasant doings, including attending a Sunday party given by a local couple, artists with a beautiful old house on a large property, who had invited the entire neighborhood. I looked forward to meeting some of my neighbors. Saturday morning, I sat down on the window seat in the kitchen with my morning tea and opened my newspaper. Suddenly, I felt a *ping* in my esophagus.

I was still on antibiotics for the infection and had to take a pill first thing each morning before eating. I thought perhaps it had become stuck, as sometimes happened with large pills, causing an ulcer to open up immediately, making me sick for two or three days. But I did not feel sick now, just terribly enervated.

I told the kids something was wrong but I didn't know what, except I felt horribly weak. Going back to bed, I slept on and off that day and the next; the kids refused to go to the party without me and spent the entire weekend hanging around the house, worrying. On Monday, an old pal from college days, Moe Schneider, stopped in to visit. I hadn't seen him in over twenty years; he was one of the friends my husband took (friends as well as possessions get divvied up in divorces) when we separated. In bathrobe and slippers, I sat up in a chair; luckily, Moe is talkative, and I did not have to say much.

After several days of trying to talk by phone to local doctors, who did not know me well enough to understand that I would not complain if something was not wrong (I can't really blame them; I was terribly vague), I finally reached Edie, who told me to go down to New York and check into St. Luke's. I packed up in despair: I had been out of that hospital for only *eleven* days. The kids drove me there, by now used to this drill too, and sat with me in the emergency room. Since I could not explain what was wrong with me, I thought I might have trouble being admitted, but they let me in swiftly because my blood pressure was so low I was about to go into shock.

Edie and Lucy at first assumed I had another kidney

infection; Dr. Lowe, the urologist, insisted I did not. I didn't enter this argument. I caught pneumonia almost immediately after being admitted, and because I had a pleural effusion, Edie and Lucy suspected a pulmonary embolus and tested mainly for that, and for cancer. They gave me a chest CT scan first, then a VQ scan (a ventilation profusion scan, in which, after an injection of radioactive dye, your breathing is tested). They did a pulmonary angiogram, which involves inserting a tube into a spot near where the leg meets the torso, working it up to the heart-lung area, and then doing tests. One is conscious during this: it is not painful, but it feels creepy. They did a thoracentesis, which involves pushing a long needle through the back, into the lining of the lung, and extracting fluid. The doctor swore it would not hurt, but it did, and I cried. I kept crying, and the poor young doctor worried that he had done me serious damage, had perhaps punctured my lung, which can happen in this test. He returned several times later that day and finally, with great relief, announced that he had not punctured my lung. I apologized for crying, for being a baby. I said I'd been too sick for too long, and now my body was like a baby's: it cried when it was hurt and I couldn't control it. I told him the spot still hurt where the needle had been inserted.

"The body remembers pain," I explained.

"So does the person inflicting it." He smiled ruefully.

None of these tests showed pulmonary emboli or cancer, so they ordered an echocardiogram. It showed that I had had a heart attack. I was in heart failure, with pleural effusion. No one had seriously thought of a heart attack because it had been "silent": I had felt only a *ping,* and it had caused no major visible event.

This hospitalization forced me to cancel a promotional tour in France, important because I had not done promo there for some years; and a side trip to Sligo, to visit my friend Lois Gould in Bertolt Brecht's old house on the Irish coast, which she had recently refurbished beautifully. I missed seeing Lois, but the cancellation of the French trip did me serious damage.

I was released from the hospital as soon as the pneumonia was gone, and Edie and Lucy put their heads together with another doctor (the sweet guy who'd done the thoracentesis, I think) to come up with the name of a cardiologist who was first-rate but whom they thought I might be able to tolerate. Apparently, cardiologists are among the least amiable members of the medical profession, known for indifference, superiority, and arrogance. My friends had difficulty reaching unanimity on anyone, and once they made a choice, I had to wait for an appointment until mid-October.

I believed them when they said I'd had a heart attack, but since I had felt a mere pinprick, I assumed it was extremely mild. So I was dismayed when I found that after rising late, making tea and toast, cleaning up the kitchen, dressing, and making my bed, I felt an overwhelming need to lie down for a half hour. I find enervation extremely disconcerting—as I did during radiation.

The cardiologist was a decent man. He sent me for a stress test, which for me—unable to walk well enough to work a treadmill—required the injection of a radioactive isotope into the blood. A scanning device tracks the isotope as it moves through the heart, to find areas where blood flow is impaired. I had this test on October 18 and saw the cardiologist again on the twentieth.

I date the beginning of my present state of being to that appointment. The doctor told me I had congestive heart failure. He suspected that the radiation had damaged my heart enough to cause the attack. There was no way to repair it. Unlike some heart ailments, it could not be helped by a bypass or plastic valves or any other surgery. Half of the heart was dead. He showed me pictures from the stress test, showing the bottom of my heart in black, while the rest was in brilliant color, fluid reds and blues and purples. I have never cried in a doctor's office, nor did I then, but I had to make a great effort to control myself that day. Because at that moment I realized that through all my disasters, I had unconsciously been telling myself that bad as everything else was, my heart was strong. My mother, who had had a silent heart attack in her seventies, had lived to eighty-two (her heart attack had been a mild one); my father was still well and vigorous at eighty-eight. I believed it was my heart that had kept me going through all the setbacks of the last two years. But now my heart was half gone, damaged beyond repair.

The doctor prescribed various medications but suggested no physical regimen for me and banned no activities or foods. He probably assumed I knew about fat and cholesterol (I did) and that if I had questions, I would ask them. But I do not ask questions if I think the answers might conflict with my desires. I mentioned only in passing that I was planning a trip abroad the next week, careful to speak in such a way that the cardiologist would not feel I was asking advice; I did not want him to tell me to cancel it. I was supposed to go to Sweden and Norway, then to Germany, to promote *Our Father*. I warned my hosts that I had had a heart attack and was not up to my former energy level; I asked them to keep my schedule light. My Swedish publisher scheduled five events plus a formal dinner each day—far less than I used to do but really more than I can do now. I didn't know that then; you discover what you can do by trial and error. My Norwegian publisher scheduled only two events plus a formal dinner, yet by the sixth day of my tour, my second day in Oslo, I was exhausted to the point of feeling sick and almost passed out during a hot, airless couple of hours signing books in an Oslo department store. But I thought I would be rested before my tour in Germany started, because I first had a week on my own.

I stayed at the Brenner Park in Baden-Baden, a great hotel with a fine dining room. Guests were given a tour of its magnificent kitchen. I am a cook but had never realized what it means to use *no* prepared foods in a kitchen—as was the case at the Brenner. They made not just their own stock for soups and the bases for sauces (as I would have expected) but their own breads and rolls and melba toast, even their own noodles. The huge kitchen was filled with men working, although the dining room never seemed crowded.

The streets of this resort town are charming, and there is a beautiful park behind the hotel, still colorful with leaves in October. I walked along its path bordering a little river, the Oos. The park extended for miles along the riverbank, with houses set back in quiet privacy. There were native walkers as well, at whom I smiled and nodded; but they returned forbidding glares. Perhaps it was the way I was dressed, although the outfit was beautiful to my eye—a heavy matching pullover and cardigan in white, navy, and fawn, with fawn pants and shoes. But the women who walked their little dogs all wore dresses, coats, hats, stockings, and semi-high heels, along with their disapproving expressions. The men, too, many with dogs, dressed as if for a formal occasion and acted aloof. I swam in the marvelous hotel pool and took chauffeured day trips through the Black Forest and to Heidelberg and Strasbourg. The countryside and villages are exquisite in this part of Germany, which seems, from the look of it, to be prosperous and to have a history of prosperity. The beauty and the wealth of the area contributed to my puzzlement over why it had been so enamored of Adolf Hitler.

When I received my German schedule it frightened me a bit. My publisher had scheduled ten straight days of promotion; she had included only one or two interviews or formal lunches a day—a far cry from what I had done on my last tour. She probably felt she was asking little, but she had scheduled a reading *every night,* as during my German tour in 1992. A reading a night may not sound like much, but it involved dressing by five-thirty to prepare, leaving the hotel about six o'clock, riding for an hour in a car to a bookstore. The reading would begin at seven-thirty and last forty-five or fifty minutes; questions from the audience would take up another half hour. Then I was expected to sign books (Europeans love signed books)—another forty-five minutes to an hour—and then drive back to the hotel. I would arrive there at ten-thirty or eleven, having had no dinner and too tired to eat—not that restaurants in rural hotels were open.

After three days of these five-hour ordeals, I feared another attack. I felt extremely enervated and weak, as I had after the first attack. The young women escorting me took me to a local clinic, by which I was pleasantly shocked. Large, airy, immaculate, beautifully furnished, and *empty,* it could not have been more different from American emergency rooms—although the ER in Fairview Hospital, Great Barrington, is often empty. In Germany, the doctor had to be telephoned at home. He arrived swiftly and greeted me with grace and charm; courtly as a Southern gentleman, he ushered me into the examining room. He did a few tests, then made a call summoning a senior doctor, who was equally gracious. After doing an echocardiogram, the two men together approached me very gently. Usually, they said, people who came to their clinic in the middle of the night citing chest pains had indigestion and were sent home. It was a rarity, but in my case, they were very sorry, they regretted deeply the necessity of telling me that I should sign myself into the hospital, as my heart was in terrible shape.

I said I knew it was bad and was planning to go home the next day. It was clear to me that if I continued to do promotion, I would die. I could not go through one more long night. The next day, I made a flurry of arrangements, feeling sorely disappointed with myself for letting the publishers down—letting myself down, for that matter. I had made one arrangement on my own, a speech at the college in Mainz. I'd been looking forward to it, but had to cancel that too.

I went home chastened and saw Edie almost immediately. When she asked why I had not told her I was going to Europe, I said I didn't want her to tell me not to go. She didn't have to advise me to keep my activities to a minimum. In the future I would listen to my body with even more attention.

The heart attack ended my days of delusion. I never again imagined that I would regain my old strength, my old body, my old energy. The extreme tiredness continued for months. Eventually, the quickness that had previously characterized my movements returned—for a year or so. Then other problems grew worse, and that energy faded. I no longer think in terms of recovery but only of small gains and getting through.

Although blood in my urine no longer panicked me, it led me to urge my urologist to remove the stent late in 1994. Knowing I was going south soon, he refused. In Florida, the bleeding became more serious, and I began to have pain during urination, so I had to fly up in March 1995 to have it removed. I had new and unpleasant urinary tract problems—an intense need to urinate just about every hour, and pain during urination. But Dr. Lowe seemed uninterested. This surprised me—he had been an extremely friendly doctor; he would stop in to visit me at St. Luke's–Roosevelt even when I was there for reasons unconnected to his specialty. He seemed now to feel there was nothing more he could do for me.

While I was in New York, I had another endoscopy

at Sloan-Kettering. It was my sixth and my *last*. When I came out of the anesthesia, Dr. Gerdes, with a big smile, informed me that my esophagus had healed. He was jubilant, and so was I, but I wondered why I still had the symptoms, still had difficulty swallowing. He explained that chemotherapy and / or radiation damages all the body's soft tissues, and that my esophagus had probably lost its elasticity, its peristaltic power. He prescribed a pill to help it, to be taken a half hour before eating. I flew back to Florida pleased with myself for my one bit of recovery.

I had this year done something I'd long wanted to do: for years, I'd talked of painting in watercolors. I had bought paints and paper during one of Jamie's visits and asked her to teach me. She claimed not to know how—she painted in oils (which did not prevent her from tossing off beautiful watercolor sketches when she sat down with the paints). I had tried it on my own, but I knew I was not handling the paints properly. So for Christmas 1993, Jamie had bought me paints, paper, brushes, a board and easel, and five lessons with her friend Ophrah. It had taken me the entire year to manage to take the five lessons, but I had very much enjoyed them.

Painting was—is—almost exactly the opposite of writing for me: I feel it to have no moral / political content (which I do not believe about anyone *else's* painting); I like almost nothing I produce (I usually do like what I write), but—and this is rare for a perfectionist—I enjoy the process enormously anyway. Occasionally, I feel I am improving; I always feel I am learning: but it does not matter. *It does not matter how well or ill I do.* I have never felt that about writing, not even when I first started to write daily. I always judged myself by my writing and put tremendous weight upon it. Painting was easy, not a burden, since poor performance did not matter.

After returning from Florida, I saw Edie, who in an effort to treat my new urinary tract problems arranged for me to see a nephrologist she respected highly, Sheldon Glabman. (It was Dr. Glabman who later wakened me, mornings at Mount Sinai, with a hand on my forehead. I had liked him before that—he is an extremely cultivated man—but that endeared him to me.) He in turn sent me to a new urologist. He ordered another sonogram, which revealed my kidney stones but showed no cancer. The urologist gave me belladonna to ease the pain, but it did so only slightly and did not reduce the frequency of urination or the bleeding at all.

I had no sooner settled in in the Berkshires for the summer than I developed pain in my side and a slight fever. I had come to expect kidney infections on holidays, and sure enough, it arose over the July 4 weekend. Thankful that my daughter was with me and could drive me to New York—I did not want to take another horrible superexpensive ambulance ride—I went this time to Mount Sinai Hospital, my new doctors' base.

Indeed, I had another kidney infection, and this time they had trouble dealing with it. After they got the infection under control, Dr. Glabman prescribed some medications that would, he hoped, dissolve the kidney stones. Why these had not been prescribed before, I do not know. He said it might take a year, but I should get rid of the stones and then have no more kidney infections.

My frequent hospital stays changed my behavior. Acting agreeable and docile was a thing of the past. On the other hand, perhaps I was never as patient and docile as I thought. Certainly Edie and Lucy thought of me as properly tough on doctors—Edie called me "feisty"—and I castigated more than a few nurses and doctors at St. Luke's–Roosevelt. But I was probably more docile at S-K.

A young Indian doctor at St. Luke's, a mere girl really, had been told to give me a TB test. It involved being stuck with a needle. The next day, she approached me with a flat metal board covered with needles, which she wanted to press into my arm. During this period, I was constantly being tested for pulmonary emboli, and I felt like a pincushion. I told her I didn't want the second TB test. I didn't like the look of the thing, and I'd been stuck enough. She insisted. I said that if I refused a treatment, that was that. She continued to insist, and I gave in, but I cried when she hurt me. If the young doctor had had any notion of what I had been through, she might have been a little sympathetic (like the guy who gave me the thoracentesis), but instead she reproached me. Weeping, I said I didn't want to be hurt anymore, I wanted to die. She was shocked.

"How can you say something like that!" she scolded, this twenty-something twit. She nodded at Rob, who was visiting me that day. "Look at you! You are a lucky woman! You have a son, and he comes to visit you! You should be grateful! A woman should be grateful to have a son! You should not say such things!"

The blast she got then blew her out into the hall. I never saw her again, but I heard about her dismay from Edie and Lucy, who wondered what had happened. When I told them what precipitated my explosion, they exchanged half-smiling glances.

Strange doctors who led processions to my bedside, expecting obedient submission to orders to examine me publicly en masse, got short shrift. But the doctors I most often reprimanded were overbearing men who bullied or were rude toward my roommates, often poor women on Medicaid. I intervened because the women accepted this treatment in silent passivity (as poor women usually do). Doctors are especially detestable to poor women of color, and I derived great pleasure from challenging this. Once, at Mount Sinai, eight men (professional visitors: they were too old to be students) stood around the bed of my roommate, a beautiful black woman in her thirties, regarding her poor carved-up body (she had had so many operations that she looked as if she'd been used for experiments). The headman told her she needed another operation. When I loudly warned her not to believe him, to get a second opinion, a young doctor in the entourage snickered. She had a parade of physicians—the same one rarely returned twice. Another day, a doctor said her pain (which she had complained about for days but that no one had treated) was in her head, and he asked how old she was. When she told him, he said, "Well, you're too young for menopause, but you're still imagining things. How is your mental health?" She looked at him in bewilderment.

I exploded. "What!" I cried. "Are you saying you think menopausal women are crazy? Is that what you're implying? Are you really so stupid and inexperienced that you believe that?"

Doctor or no, he no doubt believed exactly that. He glanced at me in deep unease, even fear, and rushed from the room. (I had just validated his assumption.) My roommate turned to me a face smiling with gratitude. The next day, she spoke up to a doctor who was treating her superciliously.

I had been working all this while on *My Summer with George,* and while I was in the hospital in July 1995, I revised it, finishing the revision the day after I left. I went back to the Berkshires as soon as I could. Again, I was weak and needed help with carrying and lifting; again, I slowly grew stronger.

In New York, on an evening late in September, after my daughter and I had seen the play *Ecstasy* off Broadway, we walked to the corner for a cab, and I suddenly found myself lying on the sidewalk, on my back. People all around were alarmed, and helpful, especially the women, but thank heavens I had Jamie to see me home. The next day, I was all right but uneasy. I called Dr. Lieberman, the Sloan-Kettering neurologist, for an appointment. He ordered an MRI, which showed I had brain damage from the chemotherapy. Luckily, the damage was to my cerebellum, not to the cognitive portions of the brain, but it was irreversible, he said, and nothing could alleviate it.

I worried for a while, fearing that I might fall down when I was out alone, hating the thought that I might need a keeper to be with me at all times. But I have fallen only once since then. This marked the beginning of a severe deterioration in my walking ability: I am often dizzy and walk into walls; I often feel I will fall, and sometimes I do collapse. I need to sit down or rest briefly when I stand or walk. But I have not again blacked out during a fall.

I had no further health crises that year, although my urinary tract problems remained.

In January 1996, I flew down to Florida. Perhaps I was more ambitious than usual, or more energetic, but I have less help in Florida than anywhere else, and things are hard for me there. In any case, I realized after a time that my back was particularly painful. I ignored this, thinking each day that I had been too vigorous in swimming the day before, that I should not have carried that half-bushel of oranges up to the apartment. In late February, I flew to England to deliver the Oxford Amnesty Lecture at the Sheldonian Theatre, thrilled to speak in that historic hall. I spent some days in London seeing publishers. I stayed at my favorite British hotel, the Connaught, which is beautiful and luxurious, with a great dining room. In addition to its exquisite meals at lunch and dinner, it manages to deliver a perfect three-minute soft-boiled egg every morning—which as far as I am concerned is the real test of a hotel dining room.

By late March, I realized that the back pain had been particularly bad for a very long time, and I consulted my Florida doctor, who sent me for X rays and a bone scan. I had suffered another compression fracture. The doctor sent me for physical therapy, but I was already being treated by an expert in craniosacral therapy, who managed to keep my pain tolerable; the supplementary traditional physiotherapy did not seem to have any added effect.

My urinary tract problems were growing ever more severe, and when I returned to New York, I again saw the new urologist. He performed a cystoscopy and found my bladder full of blood, but no sign of cancer. The next step was a CT scan, and, because I was staying in my Massachusett's house, I arranged to have it done at a hospital in Canaan, Connecticut. But the doctor had not specified whether iodine was to be injected to provide contrast in the X ray, and the technician was afraid to proceed. Not wholly trusting the urologist (who had messed up arrangements for several previous appointments), I had the technician call Edie, who absolutely forbade the use of iodine. I went home. There was no CT scan, and no further tests were done. They—Edie; the nephrologist, Dr. Glabman; and the new urologist—had ruled out cancer to their satisfaction. Edie did not want me to have iodine (which harms the kidneys and, in my case, could be fatal), so a CT scan would be of minimal use. They concluded finally that my urinary tract had been damaged by chemotherapy, that there was nothing to be done, and I would simply have to live with the consequences. This was becoming the standard answer to all my problems.

Indeed, that is the diagnosis of most of my present medical complaints. Happily, the medication to dissolve kidney stones was effective and within three months had eradicated them, as a new sonogram and X ray showed. Once they were gone, Edie made sure I was sterile (by prescribing a final course of antibiotics and testing the urine again to make sure it was infection-free). Once sterile and free of kidney stones, I had a chance of remaining free of infection. I have not had a kidney infection since and have not spent a night (although I have spent days) in the hospital in a year and a half. Consequently, I have not suffered periods of regressive enervation. I am grateful for the respite but do not consider that this means I am "better" or will recover. My walking grows steadily worse as the neuropathy progresses up my feet; the dizziness from my brain damage probably has a similar prognosis, since the effects of toxins and of radiation continue in the body for the rest of one's life.

With concentration, I can walk straight. When, distracted, I fail to concentrate on walking or standing—as happens at large parties, for instance—I become weak and dizzy and feel I will fall down. I dread that someday I may not be able to walk unaided, but that is not predictable, and I refuse to spend good years of life thinking about wretched things that may not happen. Regular Feldenkrais and craniosacral therapy for my back and arm problems enable me to stand a wee bit straighter than I did and to move my arms a bit more widely. I even have moments without pain. My heart has improved a tiny bit, as has my kidney function. The latter things have happened automatically; they are signs of the body's miraculous ability to heal itself.

CONCLUSION

SPRING 1997

After all the ups and downs of 1992, 1993, 1994, and 1995, after the heart-clutching terrors, the flashes of exaltation when I thought I was recovering, and the inevitable disappointments that followed, I reached a plateau of serenity. Years of pain, dread, and severe illness smoothed out into a quiet state of mild impairment. Nineteen ninety-six was the first year since my diagnosis in 1992 in which I was not hospitalized. Since each hospitalization had cast me back into enervation and muscle weakness, I could now stop this regression and work on growing steadily stronger. Of course, I did not know at the beginning of the year what it would prove to be like, and there were many episodes of sudden bleeding, or sharp pain that made me clutch in fear.

At present, I feel relatively well. My back aches almost constantly but not severely, except when it is tired; a regimen of medications and a low-protein diet have kept my kidneys quiet; the urinary tract problems remain, and I am bothered every hour and never get a full night's sleep, but now that I know they do not indicate cancer, they do not worry me.

A few months ago, I read Reynolds Price's memoir of his ordeal with cancer, *A Whole New Life* (1995). Price had cancer of the spine and received considerable radiation. As a result, he is now a paraplegic. He writes that severe spinal injury almost always damages the nerves controlling bladder function. Most para- and quadriplegics have trouble emptying their bladders; they often lose control of their urination and develop urinary tract infections. For months, I believed that my urinary problems, which did not begin until 1995, were a late result of radiation. Price had another problem I share: he calls it "storms" in the nerves of his back and legs, resembling an immense amplification of the pins-and-needles sensation. I have had what I always called "hard pins-and-needles" across my midriff and back since I awoke from the coma. It can be very strong and unpleasant, and arrives suddenly when I stretch an arm farther than it wants to go or move my torso quickly. My craniosacral therapist, Susan Trider, told me several years ago that as she worked over my body she felt a strange prickling sensation—although I had never told her I suffered from it. Her efforts paid off, and the sensation is much reduced now.

My walking and balance have grown considerably worse over time, but I do not fall regularly. And since I have been treated by a naturopath, Dr. Ember Cari-anna, and by Susan Trider (both in Florida), precisely to counteract the effects of radiation and chemother-apy, I have been walking better. Susan teaches a visual-ization in which the patient superimposes the figure 8 on the part of the body that is troubled. She has an original theory about this figure, about which she is preparing a thesis. The figure 8, which is of course the symbol for infinity and the shape of the Möbius strip, is also a "natural" motion: if one closes one's eyes while standing up, the body automatically moves in a figure 8 pattern. I imagine it whirling through my cere-bellum, my spinal disks, my bladder, and other hurt parts of my body. Imagining it swirling around me as I walk down halls seems to keep me straighter. One of Susan's patients, a paraplegic, began to move after a long period of doing this visualization. Susan has for several years given me craniosacral treatments when I am in Florida. The rest of the therapy—visualization of 8s, and Dr. Carianna's herbal and homeopathic remedies—is too recent for me to be able to say much beyond the fact that it *has* helped me in only a couple of months.

My present state is merely my present state—it may change tomorrow, and probably for the worse. Indeed, my urinary problems did worsen during a trip to En-gland this past June, and when I returned, I called Edie to ask her to prescribe a medication that had helped a professional woman golfer with interstitial cystitis.

Instead she sent me to Dr. Suzanne Frye, a urologist, who expects to relieve my symptoms through a hospital procedure that will not require an overnight stay. I trust her because she performed a cystoscopy on me in her office, which I barely felt; the same procedure, performed by my last urologist, had me screaming on the table. Disgusted, he told me the problem was that I was too small. But the problem was his ignorance of female bodies. I think male urologists should hang out shingles reading "Practice Limited to Men Only"; they should not treat patients whose bodies they do not comprehend, charging money, causing pain, and leaving them dangling. Since I wrote this paragraph, Dr. Frye has given me a series of treatments which have much alleviated my symptoms. I now waken only twice or three times a night, and hope for even more improvement in the future. In addition, acupuncture has increased the sensation in my feet.

I was recently diagnosed with diabetes. Since I am not overweight, do not often eat sweets, and have no diabetes in my family line, I am bewildered by this. I must limit even further my already limited diet and stick needles into myself twice a day every other day to keep track of my blood sugar. Other than that, the diabetes is of no concern. It was just one more blow to a being nearly numb to them.

Just about every system in my body has been damaged to some degree by chemotherapy or radiation. I take fourteen prescription medications every day of my life, some twice a day; and five more on occasion. I spend over a thousand dollars a month on medications, not covered by insurance. I spend more than half that amount each month on physical therapy, which I will probably need for the rest of my life. Nor is this covered by insurance. The natural remedies are cheaper: I take six of these at present. The only problem is that I take medications all day long.

I look like someone who has been sick. I aged greatly during my illness: my skin wrinkled when I lost weight and from the drying out of my body by chemotherapy; some of this faded, but some lasts. Strangers seem to recognize simply by glancing at me that I am in some way impaired; they often reach out a hand to help me. This is both gratifying and upsetting. It always makes me happy when people act helpful, kind, altruistic; but on the other hand, I dislike being continually reminded of how disabled I appear. When walking, I like to rest my arm on another's arm, for the support, not of strength, but of steadiness. I know I walk straighter if I walk with someone else. But often the people holding my arm warn me about a step coming up, and I want to snarl (like my grouchy mother in her old age), "I'm dizzy and unstable, not blind!" Sometimes I do.

It has been rumored that chemotherapy destroys one's sexual drive, and certainly that seems to be the case with me. I had already passed the time of life in which desire is fierce, most compelling (which is the best reason I know for acting on desire when you feel it: it is not a permanent part of the somatopsychic complex). But I feel it not at all anymore. Of course, nothing has provoked it recently—and at my age, it takes something powerful to provoke desire. So I can't be sure. But I am glad I let myself experience sex widely and richly while I could.

It is fortunate that I was always a sedentary person, that the activities I love are sedentary. I like to write, read, paint, play the piano, talk to friends—all of which are done sitting down. Suppose I'd been a professional golfer? Or a mountain climber? But if I had been, my leg muscles would be stronger, and different things would be wrong with me now. I'm convinced of this: what goes first in illness are the systems that were weak before. My walk was always unsteady, even when I was healthy, because I exercised my legs insufficiently as a child; kidney problems are congenital in my maternal family.

Despite everything, I retain a kind of vigor, an enthusiasm and a passion that do not diminish, even when I wonder where it is bubbling up from. This means I can have fun. I look forward to and enjoy almost everything I do in the course of a day. The things I find unpleasant (most doctors' visits—but not those to Edie Langner—waiting in a doctor's office or hospital lab, being caught in New York City traffic jams, for example) are unavoidable and happen to people who are not sick. But my years of trekking in the elephant dung have mostly ended.

In past times, it was customary for authors to beg pardon of the (usually) aristocratic patron-reader for taking up her or his time. Even a great poet like Edmund Spenser would apologize for his lack of skill, offering fervent assurances of his desire to please. Such disclaimers do not fall comfortably on twentieth-century ears, but as I finish this book, I feel a need to ask the reader's indulgence for my long recital of personal ills. I feel uncomfortably like someone who obsessively subjects others to hours of description of her latest operation. Perhaps I feel this way because although I wrote this book in the hope that others might find it useful or interesting, I also needed to write it for personal reasons.

Over the past four years, when people asked what had happened to me, I would offer a brief explanation. If they were curious and probed, however, I found myself telling them the whole story. I told it over and over. It was not the telling that was a problem; it was my bewilderment about why I *needed* to tell it and how I could tell it over and over without tiring of it. Worst of all, I wondered why I felt a knot of tearfulness rising in my throat, especially when I spoke of events surrounding the coma. I wondered if I was suppressing some unfinished psychological business.

Judith Herman writes that "unassimilated traumatic experiences are stored in a special kind of 'active memory,' which has an 'intrinsic tendency to repeat the representation of contents.' The trauma is resolved only when the survivor develops a new mental 'schema' for understanding what has happened."* She quotes Doris Lessing's description, in *Under My Skin,* of her father's stories of World War I, which "he told

*Herman cites M. Horowitz, *Stress Response Syndromes* (Northvale, N.J.: Jason Aronson, 1986), 93–94. See Herman, *Trauma and Recovery* (New York: Basic, 1993), 41.

again and again, with the same words and gestures, in stereotyped phrases" (Herman, p. 38). Although I had not reached this point, I felt that if I was ever going to be able to lay the past to rest, I must in some systematic way deal with my memories and glean the memories of the people close to me. I feel this has happened through writing this book, by what magical means I don't know.

Many people expect accounts by survivors of serious illness or accident to affirm some intuition of deity or purpose. I can offer neither of these. At no time in my illness or during my recovery did I believe that I was part of any larger purpose, a pawn in some god's plan. Nor did I feel selected for a special ordeal, as people seem to who ask, "Why me?" When people insist—always with a knowing look, an assumption of superior knowledge—that I was saved for a reason, because I am special, I think, but do not say: Does that mean that among the uncountable millions who died in Auschwitz, Hiroshima, Bhopal, or the most recent massacre by a madman with a repeating rifle, there was not one who was special? Only I am special? Only I, of all the people who develop esophageal cancer, mattered enough to save? The idea that one was saved because one is intended to accomplish something is offensive: it assumes that doing something in the world is of greater importance than simply being.

Some may protest that if there is no larger purpose to our lives, they have no meaning. But what is the meaning of statements that life has meaning, or hasn't? Why should life have a meaning outside ourselves? Is it necessary, for our peace of mind, that we fit into a scheme larger than ourselves, in which we are each little cogs contributing to the sum of good or evil? We do not even know, really, what good and evil are: it seems to me this is the subject on which humans are most deluded. The demand that life have a purpose beyond itself diminishes life. We have enough purpose for our own lives: we want to feel alive, we want certain things—not just materialities, but experiences. We want to be important to at least one other person and loved by many people; we want to use our abilities, whatever they are. We want to contribute to our little—or larger—worlds and be respected within them. We judge our lives and ourselves by how closely we have come to achieving the things we desire, by how we feel about ourselves, and most of all by the quality of our daily lives. We do not need more. To imagine a deity who resembles a schoolmaster keeping a list of merits and demerits on each human soul seems to me infantile. What would be the point of that in a world in which evil and ugliness so far outmeasure virtue that we are amazed when we discover goodness?

When we die, all we are possessed of is our experience. It is one part of our lives that is largely in our own control. We have no control over where we are born, our sex, color, or size, our intelligence and talents; we have only limited ability to change our class or economic status; and no control at all over the twists of history, which with utter caprice and randomness can toss us into a death camp, a peaceful quiet period, an economic depression, or an exciting period of renaissance. Most of us spend much of our lives simply coming to terms with the inexorable conditions of our lives. But we ourselves choose the way we take, deal with, think and feel about, and respond to those conditions. This area of life, the experiential, is most completely ours; it is what defines us and the quality of our lives. It—not accomplishment, wealth, worldly power, or fame—is the only real measure of a life. And only we ourselves can assign our lives a "grade." The richer, deeper, and more varied our thoughts and feelings, the wider and richer our interactions and connections, the richer our life. When we are old and look back, it is only this that matters. The rest is all props.

Surviving an illness or a disaster is largely a matter of luck. Although Americans in particular like to pretend that we can control our fates by not smoking, drinking alcohol, indulging in excessive sex (or the "wrong" kind)—if we exercise and eat properly, we can live forever—I find this idea superstitious. Good habits may help us live longer, if we don't die in a plane crash or from a terrorist's bomb. Yet my pre-illness habits were far from healthy, and I lived. No one knows why. The Sloan-Kettering doctors shrug off the question: they simply don't know. A hospital newsletter described me as a "miracle" patient. I asked my oncologist if he would write up my case. "No," he said. "I didn't do anything different with you than with any other patient. I don't know why you lived. I can't take credit for it."

I also reject the automatic assumption—almost universal—that life is always better than death. People cling to this belief unyieldingly and unthinkingly, but I have always questioned it, and when I was "dead," as I felt it, I liked the incredible calm and quiet—a calm far deeper than any I felt in life. When I swam up from it, or tried to sink back in it (which happened frequently after I first woke up), I was eager to return to that velvet tranquillity. Death is a friend. I still feel this to be true.

When I was about eighteen, I read André Malraux's *Man's Fate,* a novel about the Chinese Civil War that deeply impressed and moved me at the time. Of the many scenes that embedded themselves in my memory, one was of Kyo—the hero—in prison. A guard beats an old drunken man cruelly; Kyo, standing in his cage holding on to the bars, protests. The guard comes over to him and smacks his hand hard with the truncheon, or whatever he is using. It is horribly painful, but Kyo refuses to move his hands. Later, he is offered his life if he will betray his comrades. If he chooses death, he will be killed, like them, by being thrown in the tank of boiling water in a train steam engine— Chiang Kai-shek's method of killing the Communists who in good faith surrendered to him in Shanghai. Kyo chooses death.

At the time I read this, I had never questioned that life was the ultimate good. I thought about it long and as deeply as an eighteen-year-old can; life did seem to me the highest good, and I questioned those who claimed honor, or faith to a deity or a fatherland, to supersede the value of life itself. On the other hand, there are terms of life that are not acceptable, terms so depraved that they would poison whatever life was saved by accepting them. I decided then to consider moot the question of ultimate good, and I have never been able to move beyond that.

Before I fell ill, I worked for over ten years on a history of women that covered the period from prehistory to the present. In many of the societies that I described, women's lot was abominable; laws regarding women were stringent and cruel, and it seemed that so were women's lives. I was wrenched and anguished as I read and wrote about these periods, and the thought often crossed my mind that death was a blessing: at least the poor souls were now at rest.

Ordinary people rarely encounter a situation like Kyo's; ordinary people choose death for undramatic reasons that are not necessarily moral. To choose death when one is in terrible pain (physical or emotional), is old and helpless and dependent, or faces serious debilitation, cannot be labeled moral or immoral. It is a practical decision, made for practical reasons. The choice to die when one is in such circumstances is a moral decision *only if suffering is considered a moral good*—the suffering not only of the chooser but also of the people involved with her or him. And suffering is considered a good only within an authoritarian ethos, a belief that obedience to and fear of superiors, the state, or a god, is necessary. Such an ethos teaches that the individual should defer to the will of some higher power and die only when it decrees. It condemns as apostasy most efforts to take one's life in one's hands, to live by one's own will. I have rejected this ethos ever since I could think—as a life choice, not a death choice.

Moreover, the fact is that most people cling to life tenaciously. However sick they may be, in whatever pain, people continue to regard life as precious. This is a profound and almost universal truth. People who are miserable and barely able to wrench out a smile grit their teeth and insist ferociously on going on living. There is a reason why the people in the death camps were heartened by the rare suicide: although life was not worth living for the internees, they went on passively doing so. Suicide was a heroic act. It is said that Moishe Feldenkrais, who invented the Feldenkrais method of physiotherapy, went on choosing life even though he was paralyzed almost completely at the end; and a recently translated book describes the life, clung to, of a man who could move only his eyelid. Comatose, my mother clung to life for five weeks, although her last experience in life was of humiliation, as she tried to stand up and found herself tied to a chair and cried out in terror to my father to take her home. Ruth McKechnie clung to life even after they removed her life supports.

We all know of cases in which doctors say that if they remove someone from a respirator, she or he will immediately die. After much agonizing, the family finally decides to do so, and yet the patient does not die but holds on for days or weeks, comatose yet willful, clinging to life. My father-in-law, Robert French, fell ill in his thirties. He was in agony, but no doctor or clinic was able to diagnose his disease. After years of serious illness (he was unable to work, unable even to move easily, in agony when he sat up, unable to eat), he went to the Mayo Clinic. They operated and found tuberculosis of the intestines; they surmised that in France during World War I, he had eaten meat exposed to poison gas, which rotted his innards. They removed most of his large intestine and sent him home to die. He lay in an upstairs bedroom for months. Every day, a local doctor visited him. Every day, the doctor, pitying his patient's agony, said, "Bob, I'm leaving some extra morphine tablets here on the bedside table for you. If you need them, they're there." Bob never took them, no matter how terrible his pain. And one day, he rose from that bed to live for twenty years more.

I believe that most of us are like Bob French. I, having prepared myself for death, having in my rational mind accepted death, was gripped, each time I approached it, by something else, something deeper and grittier and more elemental. Some people call it will, an ambiguous term which, they say admiringly, I possess in great quantity. But I cannot take credit for something unconscious. I credit my survival of terminal cancer and a lethal coma to luck, my father's family genes, and the love of my family and friends. But clearly I wanted to live, despite my frequent aspersions on the living state.

Since most people, even those in pain of body and mind, cling to life with something like desperation, we as a race take no risk in making a means of death accessible. When I was helpless after the coma, at my lowest, speaking to my friends of wanting to die, I know (and knew then) that if I had possessed the means of accomplishing my end, I would not have used it. I spoke of death daily but made no effort to kill myself. In fact, I was making a strong effort to get better. I was negotiating with life and death.

I firmly believe that death is a friend, into whose arms one sinks gratefully when it is time. I also firmly believe in people's right to end their lives when they desire to. The argument over euthanasia in this country seems to me wrongheaded, approached in the wrong way. The question being debated is whether the populace should grant someone—a doctor or panel of doctors—the authority to decide whether a person may be permitted to die. This removes freedom from the act, which again becomes part of an authoritarian pattern. Every and any adult who expresses the wish to die should be able to obtain the means of death—a prescription, a drug, whatever. Whether people take the drug or not—or when—is up to them. I do not believe that were the means of suicide accessible, great numbers of depressed people would kill themselves in a momentary funk. Suicide is an extreme step, and one must be in an extreme state to attempt it. Moreover, I really wonder about the thinking of people who seem to assume that if death were made accessible, large numbers of people would choose it. We are intelligent enough and strong enough to be in charge of our own lives, and we all, or almost all, cling almost superstitiously to life.

Despite my daily negotiations with death in 1993, I am now deeply gratified at having lived and grateful to whatever enabled me to do so. I have no anger at the medical establishment, which may inadvertently have caused the coma and whose "cure" did cause my present afflictions. There is no malice in it; the medical establishment did for me what it could. That cancer treatment remains at a savage state is not the fault of doctors scurrying to find more benign cures.

Individual doctors can be care-less and cavalier, or caring and committed, but the medical establishment as a whole, the huge, indifferent machine, did what it could do, and by some fluke, I survived. It did what it was supposed to do, what it knew to do. Until more civilized treatments for cancer are discovered, treatment will continue to be like playing craps: toss the toxin and see which dies first, the cancer or the patient. My present problems are the payment I owe for surviving such a treatment. That they exist makes my life hard in some ways; that they are not more severe makes my survival sweeter.

Recently, a study was published in the *New York Times* suggesting that "happiness" and "unhappiness," whatever the words mean, may be genetically rooted, that people's level of contentment in life is inherent and remains the same whatever happens to them. After decades of observation, I have come to believe this is true: the things that we believe will make us happy (love imagined to be enduring and heaps of money, say) do so only momentarily, if even that. Love never endures without pain and sacrifice, and money seems to add little to human well-being. Moreover, things we are sure would make us unhappy (physical maiming, economic loss) do not hold our spirits down more than momentarily. The only loss I believe to be a permanent source of sorrow is the loss of loved people, especially children. I used to think that great poverty was catastrophic and that people with disabilities were doomed to misery and deprivation forever. I used to think that people who accomplished much in their lives were qualitatively better off than those who had not. But the most wretched people I have ever known include some of great accomplishment, wealth, and power in the world; and among the lightest-hearted people I have ever met are the utterly impoverished, oppressed, almost enslaved peasant women of India.

Still, like losing a child, a serious illness or disaster is transforming. It changes not just our bodies and psyches but the context of desire. The field from which we choose our desires shifts under our feet; we choose differently, not just because we have changed but because we see different elements to choose among. For me, the change has been profound: my happiness quotient has changed: I am happier than I have ever been, despite my handicaps.

I was never a particularly happy or lighthearted person. As a young woman, I was extremely passionate about ideas and extremely voluble about them. I rejected religion, but took seriously a passage from Revelation:

> I know thy works, that thou art neither cold nor hot: I would thou wert cold or hot.
>
> So then because thou art lukewarm, and neither cold nor hot, I will spue thee out of my mouth.
>
> Because thou sayest, I am rich and increased with goods, and have need of nothing; and knowest not that thou art wretched, and miserable, and poor, and blind, and naked . . .
>
> (3:15–16)

When I was young, each step I took out of helplessness (for me then the greatest evil) increased my satisfaction in life. Once I had work I enjoyed, I became almost content, despite a miserable marriage. And when the marriage ended, and I had work I loved, I was as close to bliss as I can imagine. Yet I was still driven, idealistically ambitious about human possibilities and angry with the world that exists. Even when I enjoyed my daily life, I lived in the future, where the ideal resided. Living in the future really means one is continually planning it, in an effort to control it—as if by thinking about it, one could make the ideal world come about. This way of being requires a belief in the future—the belief that a future exists and that one will live to see it, or at least will be able to influence it. My illness shriveled the future up and blew it away. Now I do not consider that I have a future (although I may), and I never think about it. I rarely think further than the next day. I plan only for a few months ahead (and that only recently) and always in a tentative spirit. I tacitly (silently) precede every statement of commitment by "If I live . . . if I am well . . ."

Losing the future is the best thing that ever happened to me. It altered the context of my desires, which are now limited to the present and the immediate future—that is, a few hours hence. Stuck in the present, I can devote myself to it: to daily pleasure, pleasure in the moment, pleasure in everything (or almost everything) I do. Luckily, my work has always given me huge pleasure, as do my social encounters—my children and my friends. I also love excellent food, and I do my own cooking despite my difficulty with standing for a long time. I move through the day from pleasure to pleasure like a woman walking through the halls of a great art gallery.

I no longer have large-scale desires. I no longer wish for or expect undying love, perfect harmony within my family, a life in which everything is right (which, however absurd it may be, I did desire and kept anticipating before). I have only small desires—for a glass of cold orange juice, a good book, a visit with someone I love. Not only do I have no large desires for myself; I no longer have them for the world. Coming up against the absolute limit of death destroyed my fervent belief that an ideal world could be created if only people would do x and y, believe what is before their eyes, let themselves be happier. It destroyed my absurd and unconscious belief that because I could see the ideal, I had a responsibility to help others see it, to create it. The weight of this responsibility was heavy, and carrying it made me angry. I was also angry because I was frustrated that no matter how simple it all was, it was not happening.

Coming as close to death as I did engraved on my consciousness the understanding that the ideal is not going to happen, that it was always a delusion, the daydream of a willful child, engraved upon my body by yearning and misery and helplessness like the fault tattooed on one's body by acid-dropping needles that prick it as the sinner is turned around and around on a huge rotisserie, in Kafka's *The Penal Colony*. Coming up against failure in so absolute a fashion calmed my anger and cooled my ambition. I am no longer driven. I no longer imagine that I can do much to help bring about the millennium of the humane ideal, or that I can change anything at all. I have relinquished my painful freight. I am free. I am permitted to enjoy myself. I have noticed that my laugh has changed, is more spontaneous, deeper. I am almost serene.

I cannot say I am happy I was sick, but I am happy that sickness, if it had to happen, brought me to where I am now. It is a better place than I have been before. I am grateful to have been allowed to live long enough to experience it.

A NOTE ON THE TYPE

This book was set in Garamond, a type named for the famous Parisian type cutter Claude Garamond (ca. 1480–1561). Garamond, a pupil of Geoffroy Tory, based his letter on the types of the Aldine Press in Venice, but he introduced a number of important differences, and it is to him that we owe the letter now known as "old style."

The version of Garamond used for this book was first introduced by the Monotype Corporation of London in 1922. It is not a true copy of any of the designs of Claude Garamond, but can be attributed to Jean Jannon, a Protestant printer working in Sedan in the early seventeenth century, who had worked with Garamond's romans earlier but who was denied their use because of Catholic censorship. Jannon's matrices came into the possession of the Imprimerie Nationale, where they were thought to be by Garamond himself, and were so described when the Imprimerie revived the type in 1900. The italic is based on the types of Robert Granjon, a type cutter and printer active in Antwerp, Lyons, Paris, and Rome from 1523 to 1590.

*Composed by Stratford Publishing Services,
Brattleboro, Vermont*

*Printed and bound by R. R. Donnelley & Sons,
Harrisonburg, Virginia*

Designed by Misha Beletsky